"Ted Haggard is one of those very rare people who can be relied upon to say it like it is. To turn away from revisiting the life and message of Paul—and to fail to learn these crucial lessons—would be little short of willful foolishness. Controversial and challenging, this book is a real page-turner, and the question-and-answer sessions make for equally compulsive reading. The spiritually blind or deaf will gain little from this book. Everyone else beware!"

—Dr. Clive Calver, senior pastor of Walnut Hill
Community Church, Danbury, Connecticut

"Readable. Realistic. Responsive—to God's plan first, then to people's needs. There *is* a new way to live, and Ted Haggard is a discerning, lively guide."

—Larry Crabb, PhD, founder of New Way Ministries and
author of *Shattered Dreams, The Pressure's Off, SoulTalk,*
and *Inside Out*

FOOLISH
NO MORE!

TED HAGGARD

God wants you
wise, free, and full of power

FOOLISH
NO MORE!

Seizing a Life Beyond Belief

WATERBROOK
PRESS

FOOLISH NO MORE!
PUBLISHED BY WATERBROOK PRESS
2375 Telstar Drive, Suite 160
Colorado Springs, Colorado 80920
A division of Random House, Inc.

ISBN 1-4000-7028-7

Library of Congress Cataloging-in-Publication Data
Haggard, Ted.
    Foolish no more! : seizing a life beyond belief / Ted Haggard.—1st ed.
       p. cm.
    ISBN 1-4000-7028-7
    1. Bible. N.T. Galatians—Criticism, interpretation, etc. I. Title.
BS2685.52.H34 2005
227'.406—dc22

                                                              2005005432

Printed in the United States of America
2005—First Edition

10 9 8 7 6 5 4 3 2 1

*I dedicate this book to my eldest son, Marcus Aaron Haggard.
He is a wise man who authentically understands
and lives life well. I love him, and I'm honored to be his Dad.*

Contents

a LifeGiving book

from TED HAGGARD & FRIENDS

Jesus said that He came to give His followers life—abundant life.

What an incredible promise—that any of us, regardless of the experiences of the past or the circumstances of the present, can tap into a rich, deep, never-ending supply of Jesus's *life!*

At New Life Church, we encourage the flow of this Christ-energized life into every individual and endeavor. We challenge our staff to produce life-giving ideas, life-changing messages, and life-saving advice that will equip our people to embrace the fullness of God's promises in relationships, family, small groups, church, community, and even the world.

This desire to seize all the life Jesus promised is why we joined in partnership with WaterBrook Press to produce LifeGiving Books—high-quality publications that deliver a refreshing and empowering sip of the abundant living water Christ gives to those who earnestly seek and follow Him.

Welcome to another LifeGiving Book! God bless you as you read. Here's to *Life!*

—Pastor Ted Haggard
New Life Church, Colorado Springs

Acknowledgments

In the writing of this book, I would like to thank:
- My wife, Gayle, for helping me with this manuscript.
- The church I serve—New Life Church—for allowing me the time to write.
- My family for giving me evenings with my laptop.
- My friends Ross Parsley, Lance Coles, Rob Brendle, Andrew Mondy, Kyle Fisk, Ben Robb, Meg Britton, Aaron Stern, John Bolin, and so many others who contributed ideas for this book.
- And most of all, Bruce Nygren, my editor from WaterBrook Press, who made this book possible.

One

GROWING UP

I f you pay attention, you can learn profound things about God and His ways when you're on the safe end of a Weed Eater. Just ask my sons.

Several years ago I gathered the boys for a session of yard work. It was a beautiful Colorado summer morning, an opportunity to mow grass, eat weeds, blow grass clippings off the walkways—all the landscape maintenance work that makes you sweat and gives you that healthy, tired feeling after working outside. This old farm boy loves that kind of opportunity!

I mobilized my team of four boys and headed outdoors. (My daughter, Christy, was away at her job that day and escaped this great learning experience!) At the time, my oldest boy, Marcus, was seventeen. Next in the lineup was my thirteen-year-old son, Jonathan, who is handicapped. Then Alex, age ten, and finally our youngest, Elliott, who was eight.

With my two younger sons, in order to get them to work in any way that resembled productivity, I had to use very precise instructions. After all, they were still *children*. First, I chose Alex to clean the back deck. This was justice in action, because the previous day he had gleefully sucked down a chunk of watermelon and spit all the seeds onto the deck. The rind, which he had gnawed to the white, still sat gathering bugs on the table. So I gave Alex a broom and said, "I want you to sweep the entire deck." I left him and went to assign duties to the others.

A few minutes later I came back and saw the broom lying on the floor. My man Alex was gone, but not far—I spotted him in the backyard jumping on the trampoline. The watermelon seeds had been somewhat rearranged, but the job he had done would never be labeled successful sweeping.

I had to interrupt Alex's trampolining. "Hey, Alex, let me help you with your job here." Then I showed him how to use a broom. I must say, I think it was a great demonstration of sweeping—worthy of a Home Depot seminar! But I could tell my disciple's mind, heart, and will were not engaged. Actually, Alex was frustrated with me. When I said, "Now you sweep," he showed his disgust by taking a few quick, short strokes (the opposite of my fine demonstration) while grumbling under his breath.

Now it was my turn to express my feelings. "Alex, if you don't adjust your attitude and get this right, you will be sweeping this deck for the rest of your life." Then I demonstrated a few more strokes and handed him the broom. This time Alex swung the broom wildly, flipping watermelon seeds and dirt into a little tornado. He obviously lacked appreciation for my expert advice, so I stopped him.

"Alex, this is not that big of a project, and it's not that difficult. This is basic civilization. If you can't do this, women won't love you, your children will think you are a loser, and there is not a union in the country that will let you join. No jobs at McDonald's for you if you don't learn to sweep. This is the starting point. This is A. This is only the beginning. If you can't do this, you might set a new record for incompetence. So, if you don't do this well, I will have you do it again and again. Actually, it's so important that you get this right, if you don't, you'll never eat again. You'll never sleep in a warm bed, never own a car, never listen to another CD, visit another friend, or have any kind of life except living in a cardboard box. Sweeping this deck has become your purpose-filled life, your reason for being. This is really important!"

This illustrates what preachers' kids go through. Any other dad would tell his kid to sweep the deck without using the hyperbole. But no, we preachers teach cause and effect; we teach that every misstep can alter a person's destiny. Interestingly, we even believe what we preach. Not only do I like to lecture, but I also bond with others through work. My love language is "Acts of Service," which means I connect with people by working with them. That's why doing a quality job is important to me. I also think that working as a team is vital. It can be the language families use to display their common lives. Okay, enough. Can you tell I like to preach? Back to Master Alex.

Reluctantly, shoulders slumping and feet shuffling, Alex began to slowly swing the broom and gather seeds and dust into a pile. I could almost hear the gears grinding in his head. He was figuring it out: *If I am ever going to do anything fun again, I better sweep this deck.*

Before I continue and finish the story, remember this for future reference: *Old Testament, specific instructions, law.*

More of these father-son interactions happened throughout the morning with the younger boys. I was constantly instructing and carefully monitoring: "Okay, this is how a Weed Eater works. You put on safety goggles, and you swing the cutting head this direction so the clippings don't fly back on you." I had to be very precise.

A couple of times I gave Elliott instructions for a chore and went off to work on my own jobs. Minutes later I would look back and he would be gone. I'd have to search him out, get him back on task, and encourage him.

In the midst of this beautiful Colorado morning, while Alex was learning to sweep up his own mess and Elliott was learning to do chores that would make our home more pleasant, Elliott reminded me more than once that I was ruining his life and that this was the worst day of his life. Sometimes through tears, as he was picking up paper (that, as he emphatically pointed out, he had *not* thrown on the ground), he would passionately present his case that *all* of his friends have better families than ours.

"Fine," I retorted. "This is our family, not theirs. Let's pick up the paper and clean this place up."

Ah, the sweet sounds of authentic love.

Now I knew that with a younger child, you not only have to give specific instructions; you also have to work beside him. The task can take four times longer than if you had just done it yourself. But the goal isn't solely to get the job done; it's to help the child learn how to become a competent, contributing member of the family and, consequently, of society.

Is this not a picture of how God must relate to us when we are young in our walk with Him?

But as we mature, relationships should change. With my oldest son, Marcus, my approach was different. Earlier that morning I had gone to his room and said, "Hey, Marcus. Get up! It's a great day to be alive and do yard work. I think if we all work together, we can finish in an hour or so."

"Sure, Dad," Marcus said. "What do you want me to do?"

I told him, and he astutely—if annoyingly—commented, "That's going to take much more than an hour, Dad!" He was right, of course. Don't you just *hate* that? (This reaction reveals one of many differences between God the Father and Ted the father.)

Marcus got up, dressed himself, ate the breakfast Gayle had prepared for him—eggs on toast with a slice of cheese melted on top—cleaned up his dishes, put the milk back in the refrigerator, went to the barn, selected the tools he needed, and started his work. I love this man! Not once did I have to say, "Marcus, swing the broom this way," because I'd "been there, done that" ten years earlier. And I did not have to explain the technicalities of using a Weed Eater so that he wouldn't cut off his toes. He didn't leave the lawn mower idling and slip off to shoot baskets. I didn't have to threaten, cajole, or plea with him by saying things like, "You're not going over to your friend's house until these projects are done." I didn't have to say or do anything like that to Marcus because he knows me. He knows what I want done, why it needs to be done, how to do it, and the pleasure it brings to the whole family and to our neighbors when our property is well groomed.

For future reference, remember: *New Testament, relationship, favor.*

Marcus was maturing nicely, but I knew he was still an adolescent. He was well beyond the elementary things but still not fully an adult in his relationship with me. A side story will explain why...

My wife, Gayle, and I have an agreement with our kids about cars. If each of them proceeds responsibly with his or her education and is accepted into a college we approve of, we'll buy him or her a car. When Marcus was ready, he wanted a Jeep so he could go off road, get stuck, and spin mud all over three counties—that kind of neat stuff. As his father, not totally sold on the Jeep concept, I thought, *In a year or so when he leaves for college, Marcus is going to be driving in this Jeep for hours with a couple of his friends. He will need something more comfortable than this mud flinger.*

Sure enough, after about nine months, Marcus grew tired of the Jeep and asked if we could trade it in for something else.

I said no. I told him, "This is a great opportunity in life to learn how to make a decision and stick with it." Then I gave him a sermon. (Let me emphasize, this is a compulsive behavior in my life. I have a genetic predisposition toward preaching that leaves me totally unable to stop myself. The power of this temptation is overwhelming. This is *my* purpose!) "Marcus, some people are stable and others bring suffering upon themselves. There are a few principles that benefit anyone who applies them." I took the liberty to share some of these decision-making principles with my Wise One, Marcus. He listened patiently, but you don't have to. So I'll move on.

I love my son and I want him to be happy, but I was not willing to trade that vehicle and buy him another one. Did that make me a mean dad? *Maybe.* But I don't think so. I think it made me a *good* dad. I said to him, "Look, you were excited about this Jeep nine months ago, but you don't want it now. I think you should drive it for several years. You need to make a decision and stick with it. You can't be flipping and flopping around. I guarantee you, Marcus, that if you'll learn to be grateful for this vehicle, if you maintain it well, if you'll treasure it even though it's not your dream vehicle anymore, then you will learn a principle that will serve you well for the rest of your life."

Marcus wanted me to get him a different car and use an Old Testament bring-on-the-rules-and-regs way of approaching relationships and life.

"Okay, Dad," he said, "I understand you aren't going to get me another car right now. But if I do whatever you want me to do for six months, then can I get another car?"

Oh, man, don't you hate it when your kids ask you for things in such a nice, respectful manner? But I stood firm because I love him too much to always be sweet and nice. I need to be good and right instead. So I had to give him the "bad" news: "Marcus, I may or I may not let you trade the Jeep. I don't know; I haven't got a clue now. But I know today that the least expensive car to drive is most often the one you are currently driving, so appreciate and enjoy the Jeep and we'll see what develops in the future."

The Old Testament way of "doing life" would have had me say, "Sure son, if you change the Jeep's oil on schedule, keep the carpet clean, wash it every two weeks, and don't get any speeding tickets for one year, then we'll go get a different vehicle." Marcus would have loved that, because then he would have been able to just obey my "law" and not become a man ruled by character—the kind of person Jesus said he could become. The Old Testament kind of relationship is based on keeping rules in order to please God. It is not the energized, full-of-the-Spirit kind of life Jesus modeled.

Here's the big idea: I want my son to know me; I want him to value our property in an honorable but not idolatrous way. I want him to know how to make the choices that please me and show why he deserves my trust. I desire our respect to be mutual.

So Marcus kept his Jeep. He had to earn the money to repair the damage he'd done to it off road. He started maintaining it, knowing that he might be driving it for years to come. Through this experience, he began to understand why I regularly change the oil and rotate the tires when everything on my vehicle seems fine. He developed an understanding of preventive actions. He started to understand how to keep from getting into difficult situations. He comprehended why I said that if people would obey certain principles, they wouldn't need as many miracles as those who disobey and find themselves in continual trouble. He was learning my nature, which explained the reasons behind my laws.

But as the father of a young man struggling to leave the Old Testament rule of law for the New Testament way of living, here's how I responded: I decided to watch how Marcus treated his Jeep instead of telling him how to treat it. External constraint is better than no discipline, but internal control is best. It's the evidence of New Testament life. So I took note: Did he keep the mud washed off the Jeep? Was the vehicle dirty all the time? I refused to nag, "Hey, Marcus, go get this Jeep cleaned up. This vehicle hasn't been vacuumed in weeks. Look at this! There's a hamburger crust in here that's from the dinosaur age." I didn't say things like that. I just *watched* to see what was in him. I watched carefully because he's my *child*, my *heir*. I want to bless him, but I am not going to make him dependent upon others for the rest of his life by micromanaging him. He's not been neglected. He knows. Now he's equipped to be a *man*, not a *child*, in his relationship with me.

I knew that if he wasn't respectful toward that Jeep now, five years down the road he might still be saying, "Hey, Dad, can't you get me a new car? I'm a graduate student now!" But if the Jeep was still dirty and the carpet looked like the floor in a horse barn, it would be disappointing. No doubt, I would then be tempted to say, "You're going to be driving that Jeep until you're an old man, because you haven't learned how to be grateful."

What father would want to say that to his grown son? It's this process of fostering increased responsibility that many parents—and religious leaders—don't implement, which results in their children making awkward decisions that could have been avoided. If we want our children to be exceptional adults, we need to help them grow into New Testament responsibility.

This is the point of the book of Galatians: knowing God so that our lives reflect our heavenly Father's nature.

Foolish people can obey rules and regulations, but when we are foolish no more, internal wisdom, character, and conviction dictate our actions. Paul understood this; so do good parents.

THE RIGHT PATH TO SPIRITUAL MATURITY

What I'm describing here—how I treat my children differently as they mature—is a picture of the difference between Old Testament law and New Testament grace. The Bible says, "Don't use the freedom that you have in Christ to sin" (see Galatians 5:13). Marcus had the opportunity to use the freedom he has to sin. He wouldn't be excommunicated from the family for misusing his Jeep, but neither would he get some of the pleasures he could have enjoyed. Sharing the nature of the Father's Spirit is what transforms and guides us, but it's our responsibility to grow up. If we want to stay with rules and regulations, God will allow it. We just won't ever be strong, mature, healthy people.

Living a long time doesn't guarantee insight, wisdom, or discipline. Learning as we live is what makes our future brighter than our past, which is how spiritual growth occurs. We start off as babies, which means we are helpless. A baby is fed by others, rocked by others, burped by others. A baby's schedule—when to eat and sleep—is dictated by others. To be treated like and act like a baby when you are six months old is okay. But it's pathetic when you're a forty-five-year-old man or woman still depending on others for the most basic things in life.

This is tricky because what really is babylike living is often cloaked in language about dependency upon God, submission to spiritual direction, or maybe a warped understanding of spiritual authority. No doubt, simple obedience to orders is sometimes easier, but it isn't the type of relationship parents want with their maturing children—or the type of relationship God wants with His people.

But some Christians prefer the baby state. They love going to a church that tells them everything to do so they don't have to figure out why they should or should not do certain things. They want their priest, pastor, prophet, intercessor, or evangelist to go to the mountaintop, meet with God, and then tell them what God wants them to do. Wrong. While staying connected to a healthy family of believers, they need to go to the mountaintop themselves. Simple obedience is better than disobedience, no doubt. But knowing the nature of their Father and sharing that nature is better still.

It's a gross misunderstanding of spiritual maturity when believers submit to those who tell them, "You can't understand the Bible yourself; it's just too complex. I'll read it to you and tell you what it means. Knowing God personally and deeply is a special gifting. You don't have to pray yourself; I'll pray on your behalf and hear God for you. Now you just do what I tell you to do. Go where I tell you to go. Oh, I have a word for you." And on it goes. I think this is very often a spiritually abusive situation. Maybe social services should get involved.

Yes, I'm exaggerating a little, but some Christians who follow spiritual leadership like this think that's how they're supposed to live. I guarantee, though, that they are not believers who are involved in a vibrant, energetic, life-giving relationship with their heavenly Father. The Christian life is not just obeying a spiritual leader, nor is it following the newest Christian-leadership speaker. Instead, enjoying fellowship with the family of God in a healthy, life-giving local church and listening to trustworthy leaders should help us share the spirit of the Father, recognize His voice, fellowship in His nature, and grow beautifully in Him.

Babies do grow and become children who are more capable. They learn to feed and dress themselves. With instruction and assistance, they can do simple tasks. However, their choices are very often unwise. Without a hint of guilt, a child will want to eat cotton candy and caramel corn instead of bananas and peas. A child doesn't know when to go to bed or how much sleep is necessary. A child needs to be taught how to do household chores.

What a pathetic thing, then, when someone has known the Lord for twenty-five years and still has to be told, "Okay, this is a broom. This is how you use it!" Instead, the Lord ought to be able to say to this believer, "Make the property look the way I like it. Go ahead. You are My heir, My child. You know what pleases Me. *Proceed.* You have My spirit! I'm your loving Father. Grow in this relationship with Me."

During adolescence, young people take a giant step toward maturity. Many decisions are now theirs to make. They study history and learn that there is a past, which means there is a future, too. They gain a deeper understanding of cause and effect. It's dawning on them that if they do A, it'll produce B. If they take care of themselves, they'll feel better and stronger. But if they don't take care of themselves, they are going to reap tough consequences. If they seek it, adolescents and their parents can have delightful, intelligent conversations. But adolescents can tend to take advantage of freedom by bending rules or trying to fool Mom and Dad. Imagine that—have we ever tried that kind of thing with God?

The ideal is to become an adult. An adult person is able to choose healthful food. An adult knows how to rest, understands the value of a hard day's work, and so on. An adult understands, "I'm a son or daughter of God. I'm an heir. My body is really God's property, and that requires me to act responsibly." A child needs a command, such as "Don't commit adultery." An adult says, "I understand why I need to stay sexually pure. The groom is like Christ; the bride is like the church. My intimacy with my spouse is like Christ and the church in relationship with each other. We reflect that image, so why in the world would I ever want to commit adultery?"

An adult with a childish perspective would just say, "Hey, if it feels good, do it!" A man trapped in the outlook of an adolescent would say, "I'm my own man. I'll do what I want to do."

This contrast between the Old Testament and New Testament ways is exactly what the apostle Paul had to address with the Galatian church. One group of people was saying, "We need to obey the law to show that we are *real* Christians!" But they were not in a dynamic relationship with God. Paul had to argue, "No, grow up! Move beyond the law."

Yes, the law has validity and importance. We still need to clean the deck, but we don't need to clean the deck because we fear punishment or want to finagle a reward. We clean the deck because having a deck free of watermelon seeds is nice. We know our Father, and we understand why He wants the deck clean. That's why we learn the Ten Commandments in church. However, if we obey the Ten Commandments just to obey the Ten Commandments, we've missed the point of the new covenant. The old covenant is fulfilled in the new. The deck gets cleaned; the yard gets mowed. The difference is the delight and joy of property ownership, the joy and delight of sharing the heavenly Father's values and pleasing Him. The difference is feeling the dignity of being an authentic member of God's family.

I know that if people are having trouble obeying the basic tenets of the law, threatening them with the law—punishment—doesn't provide them with the powerful inner compulsion to obey. They need to be filled with the Holy Spirit and resourced with the power of God, as well as other tools that are available, so that they can live in a way that pleases their heavenly Father.

I guarantee you, when my boys are grown, they will know how to do outside chores. I'm working to get my ways into them so they'll share my spirit, my values, and my life. I'm confident this will be true, because I learned this principle from the book of Galatians.

That's the experience the Father wants for you. God chose you to be His son or daughter, not His slave. He wants you to reflect His nature and life. God desires that you know why you do what you do, where you are going, and what you should achieve.

That's why I love God so much! He's my *Dad!* I want to think like Him. I want the kind of friends He has. I want to cut the grass like Him. I want the car to look the way He'd want it to look. I want my worship to look the way He wants it to look. And I'm not scared of Him in the sense of, "Oh, if I do it wrong, He's going to make the earth open up and swallow me." I have none of those kinds of fears.

Instead, I have a great desire to please Him so that when I walk into heaven, He'll say, "Hey, Ted Haggard's here! Good job, Ted. Well done! Let's get together." I am not interested in showing up in heaven and hearing Him say, "What were you thinking?!"

Now that I have that off my chest, let's meet the wild and adventurous apostle—Paul.

Questions for Pastor Ted

I know going to the mountaintop to meet with God is best, but I'm a mom with four kids, I home-school, and my youngest is still nursing. Can I somehow bring the mountaintop to me?

God understands the stages of our lives. For you, your mountaintop might be your faithful service to your children. God sees your faithfulness to your family and receives it as a prayer. Let me explain.

We can *say* our prayers, and we can *do* our prayers. Prayer is communication with God. We communicate with words, but more important, we communicate with actions. Preparing meals for our families communicates to God. Keeping our children safe communicates to God. In fact, everything we do is a prayer.

When an alcoholic walks past a liquor store but refuses to enter, she communicates to God that she trusts Him for restoration. When a thief walks past an unlocked car, he is resisting darkness. Actually, our actions are such strong prayers that they stimulate the presence of life and light and diminish the depth of darkness in our lives, homes, churches, and communities.

So when you play with your children, you are saying to God that you believe your children are a gift from Him. This may be your mountaintop while your children are young. Too often we look for time away from our children in order to pray for them. But the best way to pray for them is to be there when they need us.

There is a stage in life when our families consume our energy and attention. We need to grab the special moments with God for Bible study and prayer whenever we can, but don't be dismayed. God knows where you are. He sees, and He loves you loving your kids.

Two

WILD MAN FOR GOD

The apostle Paul was a passionate man. Fairly early in his letter to the churches in Galatia, he let slip how he was feeling: "I am astonished…" (Galatians 1:6). And then, not too many paragraphs later, he exclaimed, "You foolish Galatians!" He questioned their spiritual lives when he wrote, "Who has bewitched you?" which is probably one of the greatest insults Paul could have given to his churches in the region. He was concerned and angry.

Today Paul might say, "You simpletons!" or "After all I've taught you, you are still missing the point!" Here we have the apostle Paul, so deeply in love with those he reached with the gospel that he couldn't tolerate the thought of their being seduced into accepting a different gospel, a lesser gospel, or what Paul called, no gospel at all. But Paul was not a subtle diplomat. He argued his point, and he argued it with emotion. This former Pharisee, who was knocked down by Jesus and then experienced an incredible revelation of Jesus's ministry, never bothered to get up and return to the life he had known. In order to "get" this revelation ourselves, we need to meet the apostle Paul.

Let's be candid. If Paul were living today and were a member of your church, I doubt he would be the first name on your guest list for a Super Bowl party. Yes, he was brilliant, passionate, opinionated, decisive, powerful. He was also a sold-out follower of the Lord Jesus—and totally devoted to advancing the kingdom of God. But I'm not sure he was very pleasant to be around. Paul had some rough edges and some personality tics that might have made you want to sit on the other side of the room. Therapists undoubtedly would have had a field day trying to figure out why he was so "angry"—perhaps the "father-Pharisee wound"? I'm willing to bet that if Paul did drop by your Super Bowl party and saw a woman on the tube show a breast during the halftime show, he might just pick up a log by your fireplace and heave it into your new widescreen plasma HDTV. Paul was the kind of person who would come after you if he thought you were wrong about something.

In that respect Paul was much like Jesus.

And like his Lord, whom he adored, Paul had a tender side. He understood authentic love. He knew that to love others is to live for their good, to say and do what benefits them. His letters were full of genuine affection. His relationships were deep, authentic, and productive. He deeply loved the church and its people, and he knew that being firm could hurt their feelings or threaten their relationship with him. But love prevailed. When he knew their foolish ideas and irresponsible behavior would cost them dearly, he was a faithful friend who would speak up and take action. True love has a tough streak, doesn't it?

Like you and me, Paul the apostle was a product of his early-life training and experience. He grew up in Tarsus, a city in what is now southern Turkey. During Paul's life, Tarsus was a sophisticated center of learning comparable to Athens and Alexandria. No doubt Paul's keen innate intelligence was enhanced by a superb education in Tarsus.

Paul's father was a Pharisee, and Paul followed in his dad's footsteps by becoming a Pharisee too. Pharisees were very loyal to God's laws—all of them. In fact, they loved God's laws so much that they went to great lengths to obey them. They even made up some of their own rules to enhance the ones God gave in order to ensure complete obedience. The Pharisees seemed to know that their rules could enforce outward obedience but couldn't transform people's hearts. As a result, their teaching emphasized appearances more than heartfelt devotion, which, as you might recall, incurred the wrath of Jesus.

Because of Paul's loyalty to the law and to the Jewish faith in general, he became a huge opponent of the followers of Christ, who were members of a growing religious sect within Judaism called "the Way." This burgeoning movement *appalled* him.

In the early days of the New Testament era, believers were considered heretics and, consequently, criminals. In fact, Paul was so convinced that Christians were dangerous, he tried to catch, lock up, and kill as many of them as possible. He was on a Christian hunting expedition near Damascus in northern Palestine when he had his dramatic encounter with Jesus and was converted (see Acts 9). Before this, Paul had witnessed—and probably encouraged—the stoning death of Stephen, the first Christian martyr. It's important to understand that Paul was passionate for God before and after his conversion. His desire to serve God didn't change. But his understanding of how God works among men did.

So we see Paul's bold, aggressive personality reemerge immediately after he became a Christian. After three days of blindness, which was a result of his encounter with Jesus, Paul was filled with the Holy Spirit, healed, and baptized. A few days later, after eating again and gathering his strength, Paul immediately began to preach about Jesus.

(I love this guy! He never stopped; he just switched sides!) No waiting for a call and then going off to seminary for Paul. His heart was
on fire with this new revelation of Jesus as the Messiah, and since he
already knew the Scriptures, he was *ready*. And he was *good!* The
people listening to him were astonished by what he said and how
clearly he showed that Jesus was the long-awaited Messiah.

We need to note that Paul did not zip off to Jerusalem to hit the
Christian talk-show circuit. No doubt he was tempted. That the
notorious "bad boy" Paul had become a Christian must have made
him a huge celebrity in the first-century church. (Today it would be
sort of like Ted Turner, the owner of CNN, sports teams, and other
businesses, and a vocal anti-Christian, announcing that he was born
again and was studying to become a Southern Baptist pastor.)

The tables were now turned. Paul was so talented and convincing
in his defense of the gospel that the Jews in Damascus wanted to kill
him. In fact, he had them so riled up that he had to escape by being
lowered over the city wall in a basket (either he was a very small man
or the Longaberger baskets were huge back then). (Paul experienced
many life-threatening situations during his apostolic ministry, several
of which are recorded in the book of Acts.)

After this unique elevator ride in Damascus, Paul went to Arabia
and then later returned to Damascus. It wasn't until three years after
his conversion that Paul finally went to Jerusalem, primarily to meet
with Peter. While there, he also saw James. Paul later wrote of this
event: "I went up to Jerusalem to get acquainted with Peter and stayed
with him fifteen days. I saw none of the other apostles—only James,
the Lord's brother" (Galatians 1:18-19). Paul had a few tense moments
with some believers who belonged to the party of the Pharisees when

they demanded that Gentile believers be required to obey the Law of Moses.

We must remember that Paul understood the gospel and how it impacts people—both Jews and Gentiles. Since he was extremely intelligent and had a vast understanding of the Jewish law and the Hebrew Scriptures, his own dramatic conversion experience and his ongoing walk with the Lord Jesus infused life into his convictions. Paul knew Christ intimately and had tasted the liberating freedom and power of the gospel. The Christian life was not exclusively an academic exercise for him; it was an uplifting, power-packed, personal relationship with Christ.

It wasn't until fourteen years later, and after an incredible, ultimately world-changing amount of mission work, that Paul returned to Jerusalem to defend his view of the gospel message and his ministry to the Gentiles. Paul met privately with the church's leaders and said, in effect, with great energy, "Men, I received this *revelation*. This is a big deal! We *must* get the gospel right. We must be sure about what we are really saying. What truly saves a man or a woman from a Christ-less hell? How is it that we are really crucified to ourselves so that we can live the life God has for us?"

I suspect that a lot of what Paul told them is much like what we read in the book of Galatians.

Spiritual Dynamite

At just what point in his ministry Paul wrote Galatians is debated by scholars, but I tend to agree with those who say it was the last letter he wrote. This makes sense because the letter overflows with a near desperation to communicate. Paul wrote with righteous—maybe even a little unrighteous—anger because not only was he defending the gospel, he was trying to prevent years of blood, sweat, and tears that he had invested in building believers from being wiped away. In his letter he argued that the core of the gospel must be protected, no matter the cost. And now, two thousand years after Paul became so incensed and blasted this pointed letter to his followers and friends, we are still studying Galatians to comprehend its revolutionary message.

Galatians does stand apart in specific ways from other Pauline letters, such as Ephesians and Philippians. Don't get me wrong, they are wonderful epistles, but Galatians is uniquely charged with spiritual dynamite. It has been described as the "Magna Carta of Christian Liberty." The message of grace and salvation by faith alone is so important that it literally changed how the early believers viewed God, and it opened the door for Christianity to become a global religion, not just a Jewish sect. The apostle Paul deeply understood the true liberty that comes only from the Lord Jesus.

Paul wrote his letter to the churches in Galatia, a region in what is now Turkey. (Antioch, which you'll read about in the book of Acts, was an important city in this area.) Prior to Paul's missionary endeavors among them, the Galatians had worshiped Greek gods, such as Zeus and Hermes. The Galatians were pagans who didn't know the living God. Then along came the apostle who said to those living in this region, "*Hello!* You are worshiping dead idols. But for the asking, you can have a personal relationship with the real God. You can have Jesus as your Lord and Savior. You can have the power of the Holy Spirit. You can have changed lives. What are you waiting for? Believe, receive, and become new people."

Many of the Galatians who heard this must have thought, *Wow! Jesus's blood can cleanse my conscience. I can be full of the Spirit of God Himself. This is wonderful!* These Gentile Galatian believers bought into Paul's teaching and said, "We're going to believe it; we're going to go for it!"

And as Paul had promised, the Galatian Christians were having a wonderful time celebrating their freedom, finding deliverance from evil in their lives, and receiving healing. They expected God's power to work, and it did. They were experiencing the fruit of the Spirit in mighty ways.

When the leaders of the church in Jerusalem heard about all this, they were concerned and sent a fact-finding delegation to Galatia. Was something amiss up there? That's when the trouble started. These visitors from Jerusalem were born-again Jews—quite different from their born-again, saved-from-paganism brothers and sisters in Galatia. So, drawing from their background and point of view, the Jewish born-agains started giving the Galatians a list of requirements for holy living: "You are not obeying the precepts of God's Word. You need more standards. You need more character. You are not doing enough. *You* need to demonstrate the covenant that you've accepted and be *circumcised!* (You can imagine what a hit that one was!) Since you are one of us now, you need to memorize the Ten Commandments and be sure to obey them!" (See Acts 15:1.)

This invasion of Galatia by these messengers from the Jerusalem church—often called Judaizers, who loved the law and loved redemption in Christ but didn't minister life or power—brought only dry ideology and lifestyle guidelines. We have people like this in the church today. They are sincere, often well educated, seemingly godly people who want to protect the dignity of God's Word but are not experiencing the life-giving message Paul so earnestly promoted.

Just as many of the churches in our generation receive and teach this law-oriented message, so did the churches in Galatia. Paul didn't see the influence of the Judaizers as helpful; instead, he saw their message as bewitching. He saw it as a different gospel altogether. He saw it as powerful but lacking the power of God. Maybe Paul was confronting a very subtle but attractive alternative to the gospel. Maybe the reason he reacted so strongly was that this "different gospel" might, in fact, pass for authentic Christianity in many leaders' minds.

Was this "different gospel" weak? No.

Was it powerful? Yes.

Godly? No.

Did this "other gospel" have the appearance of godliness? Yes. Maybe this is why the book of Galatians is for us today.

The Galatians, in their innocence and openness to their newfound faith, were seduced. They were aware that their spiritual father, Paul, was also a converted Jew. So it made as much sense to them to express their faith by servitude to the law as it does to some of us today. Too bad they didn't run that by Brother Paul first.

When Paul found out what was going on, he flipped out. I imagine that with considerable haste he called in his scribe and ripped off a letter. His anger at those who were adding to the gospel was probably matched only by his frustration with his spiritual children. "What are you thinking?" his letter shouted at them. "No way! Not going to happen! Not in my lifetime!"

The rest of this book will explain why Paul was so agitated and will offer Paul's corrective teaching. But before we get to that, a little more general background on Paul's letters—including Galatians.

PAUL THE WRITER

The epistles of Paul are not like most of the books in the New Testament, such as the gospels of Matthew, Mark, Luke, and John. These books tell the story of Jesus and present the good news. They're broad-based documents that people from various cultures can still read to learn the primary truth. But that was not the purpose of the apostle Paul's letters.

Reading his letters is like peeking at somebody's private mail. We are at a disadvantage because we don't have the letter or the message he was responding to. All we get is one side of a dialogue. Somebody had contacted Paul and said, "You won't believe what's happening here at such-and-such church." Then Paul collected his thoughts and wrote a letter in response. And now we have two thousand years of Bible scholars' speculations about what the letters sent to Paul must have said to generate such a response from him. And, frankly, it's all just well-educated guesswork.

Although Paul's writing was fully inspired by God, I doubt that he ever sat down at a table with his pen and a piece of paper to write a tome, carefully choosing every word, and if one wasn't quite right, marking it out and putting in another word. He did not write letters with a word processor the way we would today, revising several drafts to make sure every sentence was complete and every idea well rounded.

I can't imagine Paul stressing out and agonizing over multiple drafts of his letters like a doctoral candidate in religion. He was not trying to "write the Bible." Instead, Paul wrote heartfelt messages full of truth to people he loved supremely. I think it is more accurate to imagine the apostle Paul holed up in a small room alone with a scribe or somebody who could write for him, because Paul probably had eye problems and other physical difficulties.

In this instance, a message or letter had come to Paul from the Galatian region. What he heard or read horrified him and made his blood boil. Paul was such a vigorous man, I can picture him dictating to the "Galatian fools" while pacing back and forth, saying aloud what he was thinking about each topic. With a brilliant guy like Paul, I imagine that the ideas came quickly and pointedly. I feel sorry for the poor scribe, writing like a maniac, dipping the stylus repeatedly into an inkwell, ink splattering here and there, as he tried to catch the waterfall of material spilling from Paul's tongue. The apostle had a lot to say. That's why Paul would speed along on one topic in his letters and then divert to a whole different subject briefly, then just as quickly zip back and complete the original thought. I can imagine the poor scribe in today's world, suffering from carpal tunnel syndrome, filing a workmen's-comp. claim, and needing physical therapy—but back then, he probably just asked Paul for healing prayer!

In Paul's letters you'll sometimes see a parenthetical statement in the middle of a paragraph about a different topic than the one he is currently discussing. Paul seems to stop and say, "Oh! That reminds me," and then he expounds—often in just a sentence or two—a profound insight that dramatically influences how we think or behave even today.

As I mentioned earlier, Paul passionately loved the church. As a result, all of his heart and emotion were poured out in his letters. You see the warmth in his heart for Timothy, Barnabas, and others who ministered with him.

Paul also had the other kind of feelings about people he did not get along with or just plain did not like. Paul was so passionate for

Jesus that anyone tampering with truth became an *enemy* of the faith. Paul was not always "nice," in the syrupy, say-anything, agree-with-anything way we see too often among Christians today. Paul thought there were ideas worth fighting for, and because he cared so much and battled sin like the rest of us, he sometimes got angry and had fights with people. He could be jealous, and because he had strong opinions about nearly everything, Paul was no stranger to conflict.

So how was he different from most of the "fighters" in Christian circles today? First, he was an apostle, and second, the power and fruit of the Holy Spirit were incredibly evident in his life. He wasn't just a man of ideas and beliefs. He also was a practitioner of the Word of God, building churches and demonstrating God's love for people through powerful ministry.

Take Apollos, for example. Like Paul, he was a very popular speaker during the New Testament era. (See Acts 18:24-28.) Apparently Apollos was a great-looking guy and an eloquent speaker. He would have made an excellent senior pastor of a megachurch! (Oops.) Paul wasn't the *GQ*-model type (What's that? My editor stuck it in.) and had no future as a motivational speaker.

Here's an unsubstantiated "Haggardism"*: *I don't think Paul really liked Apollos, but because of the politics of the day (Yes, Virginia, the early church had politics too.), he had to say some good things about Apollos.*

Subtly, though, Paul was warning the church not to get sucked in too much by this persuasive speaker. At the same time, Paul didn't want to go too negative on Apollos, so we see him raise a red flag of warning without saying anything specific.

---

* A *Haggardism* is an idea or saying that may be 100 percent true or equally as wrong. I think the idea is true, though, and I'm willing to stand behind it—sort of.

Paul was not proud or unrepentant, however. Why did he call himself the "worst" of sinners (see 1 Timothy 1:15)? Was he just saying that because it sounded holy? No, I think Paul was quite aware of his faults and sins, but he also knew whom to go to for forgiveness.

What, then, is the real story behind Paul's letters? I think that when the apostle Paul wrote, he never dreamed these epistles would become Scripture. I think he knew he was writing under the inspiration of the Holy Spirit, giving specific instructions about specific problems to a specific group of people. I think he would have been seriously embarrassed if he'd known anybody other than the recipients might read some of the things he said in his letters.

Paul obviously did not know—or did not care—about another Haggardism: *There's no such thing as a secret.*

For example, when he wrote to the Galatians, he had no idea that the brothers in Jerusalem would ever read his comments about *them!* If he had, at least he might have toned down his vocabulary. Paul used graphic, earthy language at times when describing his personal enemies or the enemies of the gospel. He had an incredible ability to cut to the chase and get straight to the point. In fact, it's partially because of Paul's spicy language that English Bible translators have had to cautiously choose English words that can be read in church services. Don't you just love the guy?

And so we are in for a tasty treat as we receive the insights Paul communicated in his letter to the Galatians. When we think of the book of Galatians, the word that comes to mind most often is *grace.* No doubt grace is the major theme in this letter, but Paul also had much to say about a number of other issues. (He will never be accused of writing Bible "lite"!) He addressed worship, morality, and the family. He talked about workplace issues between employees and employers.

He discussed suffering. He dealt with love a lot—and hate, too, a topic he understood firsthand because some of his enemies were vicious. Of course he talked about walking in the Spirit and the fruit of doing so. And much more.

I'm ready to dive in. But before we do, let's pray:

Heavenly Father, thank You so much for men like Paul who saw You, heard You, and obeyed You. Lord, let his letter speak into our hearts. We submit to Your Word, and we desire to be instructed by the Holy Spirit as we study. Teach us and train us to do what You do, say what You say, and go where You go. Let Your Word be written in our hearts so we can walk in joyful obedience to Your plan for our lives. In Jesus's name we pray. Amen.

Questions for Pastor Ted

Paul's writings were fully inspired by God, yet you wrote that he was also an opinionated and passionate guy. He even showed anger at times and was possibly a little "unrighteous." So when we read and study his writings, how do we discern when he is expressing a personal opinion and when he is dealing with biblical absolutes. Can opinions be divinely inspired?

The miracle of Christianity is that it is about God's working within humanity. This explains why the Bible is not a neat, systematic theology, but rather a series of stories about human beings dealing with God. Some of the stories are pretty clear, but others are messy and complicated. It's the same with the apostle Paul. While reading his letters, we can be confident that everything he wrote in the Bible was breathed by the Holy Spirit. We can also see that God was at work in the midst of very human situations. The paradox you highlight in your question is also evident in the lives of Abraham, Isaac, and Jacob. It takes wisdom to interpret the meaning of their experiences with God.

This issue is actually part of the point of the book of Galatians. Our faith is not just a series of principles we adhere to; it's the personality of God working within us. It's a wonderful adventure. It's a relationship. It's fun and terrible, easy and confusing, all at the same time. Enjoy!

What do you think the apostle Paul would both like and dislike about our local churches today?

It's interesting that churches today seem to fall into three categories, two of which are lacking in significant ways. The first category is *theo-*

logically liberal churches. These are often characterized by doubts regarding Jesus and His identity, questions about the integrity and authority of Scripture, and little or no emphasis on the necessity of being born again. Even though these churches often characterize themselves as "mainline," I have found that many of their members are, at best, cultural Christians. I don't think the apostle Paul would be pleased with this type of church on at least two counts:

- *They lack spiritual power.* In 1 Corinthians 2:4-5 Paul said, "My message and my preaching were not with wise and persuasive words, but with a demonstration of the Spirit's power, so that your faith might not rest on men's wisdom, but on God's power." These churches typically emphasize the importance of "wise and persuasive words" and have developed theological constructs that seem to disallow the "demonstration of the Spirit's power."

- *They lack decisive resolve.* In Romans 4:20-21, Paul used Abraham as a positive example for New Testament believers when he wrote, "Yet he [Abraham] did not waver through unbelief regarding the promise of God, but was strengthened in his faith and gave glory to God, being fully persuaded that God had power to do what he had promised." Certainly, mainline churches will discuss the promises of God, but they are not currently known for powerful faith. Many of their original founding principles were rooted in great faith and strong exhortations to encourage believers to receive the promises of God. But the passionate proclamation from liberal pulpits of these biblical exhortations has cooled.

The second category of churches does embrace and teach biblical truth with conviction. These are what I call *evangelical, life-giving churches.* Most of these churches have a high view of who Jesus is. With no hesitation, they emphasize Christ as Son of God, Savior, and Lord. Many of them also emphasize that He is our Healer. Not only do life-giving churches emphasize a living, dynamic, and powerful Jesus, but they are unwavering on the authority of Scripture. Second Timothy 3:16-17 says, "All Scripture is God-breathed and is useful for teaching, rebuking, correcting and training in righteousness, so that the man of God may be thoroughly equipped for every good work." In most evangelical churches the pulpit is at the center of the sanctuary in order to emphasize the centrality of God's Word—the Bible—in faith and practice.

Life-giving churches also teach the necessity of being born again. In order to have the life of God living in us in a vibrant way, we need to be born of the Spirit. In 2 Corinthians 13:14, when Paul said, "May the grace of the Lord Jesus Christ, and the love of God, and the fellowship of the Holy Spirit be with you all," he was emphasizing the importance of the characteristics that are only available when we are in a personal relationship with Christ. From Genesis to Revelation, living in the life of God is at the center of the Bible message. Without the indwelling of the Holy Spirit, which is available only through being born again, Christianity is merely mental assent to godly principles instead of a personal relationship with God. It's important to note that we are Christians not only because of what we believe but also because of the transformation that occurs when we are born again by the life of God and, as a result, know God personally. Life-giving evangelical churches accurately reflect the life and joy that Jesus and Paul intended at the birth of the church.

The last category of modern churches is what I call *tree-of-knowledge-of-good-and-evil evangelical churches.* These are churches

that have a high view of Christ and the Word and know the importance of being born again, but they are not life giving. Instead, they
are usually high-minded toward other streams in the body of Christ.
They often use the Bible as a harsh weapon of judgment instead of
drawing life from it. The differences between a life-giving church and
a tree-of-knowledge-of-good-and-evil evangelical church are subtle. A
life-giving church is characterized by an atmosphere, an attitude, and
a tone within which the Bible and the Spirit of God work.

The clearest distinction between the two types of evangelical
churches is in Genesis 2–3 where Adam and Eve had to choose between the tree of life and the tree of knowledge of good and evil. No
doubt, the knowledge of good and evil is appealing and satisfying to
people who want to be godly—and such knowledge can make us *look*
godly. But when we ingest this type of thinking, we find ourselves separated from life-giving fellowship with God and begin to judge and
blame others, just as Adam and Eve did.

In the book of Galatians, Paul was in conflict with people who
loved the Scriptures, but some of these people had become poisonous.
They were caustic. Thus, Galatians encourages us to be foolish no
more. In other words, we should gain the wisdom to embrace the life
God offers and the insight to know that we might, in fact, be foolish
enough to embrace the appearance of godliness that is deadly (the tree
of the knowledge of good and evil). When we do that, we might end
up being the fools Paul was warning others about.

Three

THE "S" WORD

Josh McDowell understands the importance of not being foolish.
I smile every time I think of this experience: A few years ago I
was in Florida speaking at a Teen Mania conference, and after giving
a talk, I went to the greenroom where speakers hang out. Josh
McDowell was sitting there, and after saying hello, I sat down to con-
verse with him for a few minutes. We chatted pleasantly about various
ministry matters and were catching each other up on our lives, when
out of the blue Josh looked me in the eye and asked, "Are you being
faithful to your wife?"

"Yes, as a matter of fact I am," I answered.

"That's great," he said, and then without offering any explana-
tion, he resumed the conversation. I wondered for a minute why he
had asked me that, but later as other speakers dropped in, I noticed
Josh did the same thing with them, too. It was entertaining—much
better than television—watching Josh launch into a "Hi, how are
you?" conversation and then drop the "Bunker Buster" bomb question, "Are you being faithful to your wife?" No one answered no, but
some were obviously shaken by Josh's bluntness.

I know Josh was not just trying to amuse himself between giving his talks. He understands the huge deal that sin is, even in the lives of "spiritually elite" Christian speakers.

And sin is a big deal for you and me, too.

Before I discuss all the wonderful "grace-full" news found in Paul's letter to the Galatians, I think it would be smart to review why, ultimately, the good news is so good: It's because of the problems caused by the "s" word. Today, when just about anything goes concerning how people behave, "sin" may be the most taboo word of all.

Years ago I was led to the Lord by Bill Bright when he spoke at Explo '72. I was one of eighty thousand teens in the stadium the night Dr. Bright spoke, and I've admired him ever since. Just prior to his homegoing, I was spending some time in his home in Orlando, Florida, and asked him if he had any regrets. He said one regret was that he hadn't spoken enough about the fear of the Lord. His concern was that although his ministry was incredibly effective at reaching people like me, his message hadn't adequately reminded people about eternal judgment and the fear of God. Sin, repentance, and avoiding the wrath of God were important concepts in Dr. Bright's life and theology, but in hindsight, he felt that he had not articulated them as strongly as he would have liked.

I believe Dr. Bright had the right message for the right time in the life of evangelicalism in the world for his generation. But I do think that now we as a body of Christians have to grow past the basics of being born again and embrace the other substantive messages in Scripture. To shun discussions of heaven and hell and judgment and sin doesn't help seekers find truth. Every human being on earth is sinful and needs a Savior. We don't do anyone any favors by acting as if this were not true. But we don't communicate this message with passion because, for too many of us, sin does not have that bad of a reputation.

Oh, we say the spiritually correct things about sin—how "God hates it," how "it's bad for us," how "it needs to be confessed," and so on. But do we really *hate* sin? Do we shudder at the ugly ramifications of sin, or do we explain it away. Sin and its consequences truly are humankind's only problem!

Here is one of my favorite Haggardisms, which I often say to my congregation: *Sin will*

- *take you further than you want to go,*
- *keep you longer than you want to stay, and*
- *cost you more than you want to pay.*

Men and women were created by God, who gave us very explicit instructions on how best to "do life."

Above all, He tells us, *"Don't sin."* Sin messes us up. Why? Because sin is living contrary to God's plan for our lives. It's forfeiting the destiny He has for us. It's going in a direction we were not designed to go. It just doesn't work as it should. Sin is neglecting God's ways—which we were created for—and choosing our own.

Certainly, our sinful choices may sound reasonable to us and look appealing at the time, but they neither work as we hope nor deeply satisfy us. Sin is rejecting God and choosing another lord that offers a shallow kind of gratification that is only temporary.

True, the Bible does say there is worldly pleasure in sin, but it lasts only "for a short time" (Hebrews 11:25). In my experience, a very, very short time. It just doesn't deliver on its promises. Every week I talk to people who have been devastated by the aftermath of sin. They would agree that pleasure is short, and the bitter outcomes are very long.

For example, a married Christian man or woman becomes infatuated with another person. The warning of the Holy Spirit is ignored, and emotional intimacy occurs—followed by one or more physical liaisons. Soon after, reality hits like a cold rain. Now, secrets must be protected with a web of lies. Then come guilt and shame and anger. Hurtful confrontations with a spouse are just around the corner. Ahead are tears and broken hearts. Children lie wounded in the ditch. The marriage may die. The man or woman might lose a job. A whole lifetime of embarrassing conversations looms. On and on it will go— the stinking garbage of a rotting sin. Who in his or her right mind would describe this as a pleasurable way to live?

An old maxim says, "A lifetime of good living can be destroyed in ten minutes of sin."

It dawned on me several years ago that sin creates community impact. I think it's important for us to ask the question, "How much is my sin going to cost others?" As of this writing, there has been only one time when U.S. Intelligence knew without question exactly where Osama bin Laden was and how long he was going to be there. The military was ready to launch missiles to remove him, but President Bill Clinton didn't execute the order because he thought that his difficulties with Monica Lewinsky would make people believe that he had launched the strike to distract attention from the congressional hearings rather than to remove a dangerous foe.

How much did the Monica Lewinsky affair cost the families of the 9/11 disaster? How much has that sin cost the soldiers fighting terrorism today?

If a dad sins, his wife and kids pay. If a child sins, the family pays. If a president sins, the nation pays. When citizens sin, their communities pay. If a business owner sins, all of his or her employees and customers pay. When employees or customers sin, the business pays. If a church leader sins, everyone within the church's influence pays. When members of a congregation sin, it drains the entire church of its strength.

Sin is like a rock hitting a pool of water. The ripple keeps getting larger and larger. The price keeps growing, and the effects reach further than we imagined.

Fortunately, there is no need for anyone to live a life wrecked by sin. Early in his letter to the Galatians, Paul said something about the Lord Jesus that is very, very important:

> [Jesus] gave himself for our sins to rescue us from the present evil age, according to the will of our God and Father, to whom be glory for ever and ever. Amen. (1:4-5)

In other words, Jesus is the answer to our sin problem. He liberates us from its power to ruin our lives.

One of the goals of Paul's ministry was to make clear that sin need not dominate anyone's life. Both Jesus and Paul knew that this earth is Satan's territory and is therefore evil, but even though we Christians live behind enemy lines in a place controlled by evil forces, the followers of the Lord Jesus are not obligated to think and function like the people who are consumed by sinful appetites and the affairs of this world. That's a big part of the gospel message Paul was so passionate about promoting and protecting.

WHAT IS SIN?

We know the basic story of why Jesus had to shed His blood and die on the cross—to forgive our sins, right? Yet I don't think we talk enough about dealing with the sin we face on a daily basis.

I define sin as "missing God's best plan for your life." Yet, that's a marshmallow way to define it. I do it because of the hyperparanoia today about the "s" word. It's crazy, but using obscene four-letter words these days often won't get you in nearly the kind of trouble that using the word *sin* will. If you don't believe me, try slipping the word *sin* into your daily conversations. If you work in the women's department at JCPenney, for example, how do you think a customer will react if you say, "I think if you wear *that,* you will be *sinning* against the men in your life!" Or the next time you are at the supermarket, tell the manager—preferably in a loud voice—"You need to get these trashy magazines that glorify *sinners and sin* off these checkout stands. *Shame on you!*" I think you get the picture.

The sin dilemma is multifaceted.

All of us at one time or another have either done or said the wrong thing. And no doubt every one of us has wrestled with right and wrong—and have chosen wrong. So we recognize that we have sinned. We have gone our own way and done our own thing. But there's even more bad news about sin. First, because Adam and Eve rebelled against God and sinned by consuming fruit from the tree of the knowledge of good and evil, and since we are their human descendants, sin is in our very makeup. Whether or not we have committed a sin, sin resides in us. We are, in our core, predisposed toward sin. We are sinners. We sin naturally. It's not a learned behavior.

So when someone says, "Gosh, I can't seem to help myself. I just lie or steal or cheat on my spouse," in a sense, he or she is showing refreshing honesty. We all are natural at sinning because it's who we are; it's what we do—as effortlessly as breathing. Do you believe that about yourself? Do you also believe it about your neighbor who is always baking cookies for neighborhood kids and sews gloves for the homeless?

External constraint, the law, can limit the number of sins we commit, but it can't keep us from being sinners. The representatives from the church in Jerusalem wanted to help the Galatians limit the number of sins they were committing, but Paul knew that their method lacked the power to change the Galatians on the inside. Paul wanted more than external constraint in the lives of the Galatians; he wanted internal transformation.

I find that many people today have an enormous struggle over specific acts of sin because they've not really appropriated the full cleansing power of Jesus's shed blood for defects in their core human nature. Why are we twenty-first century sophisticates so uncomfortable with the idea that even nice people are capable of doing bad or horrible things and fouling up life for themselves and others? Why do we hear someone say on the news every few days, "But they were such *nice* people. I can't believe they could have committed such a horrible crime"?

My answer is not the whole story, but it provides valuable insight into why we have such a hard time understanding sinful behavior.

About fifty years ago, some theories that were eventually labeled "humanistic psychology" profoundly influenced the way human beings are viewed. This ideology advanced the notion that people are basically good but get messed up by other people and life experiences. Perhaps as a result of these ideas, a new approach to behavioral standards emerged. Simply put, humanists promoted the view that most standards are random and unnecessarily create guilt, and guilt messes people up. The solution: Eliminate standards to get rid of guilt, and once guilt is eliminated, people will be healthy.

Humanists believed that eliminating standards would lead to health and wholeness. But Jesus said that when we appropriate God's power and grace, we fulfill His standards and thus eliminate guilt, which leads to a clear conscience and true wholeness.

The difficulty with the humanist's approach is that it violates our Creator's guidelines and therefore doesn't work.

A contemporary example of this kind of thinking is the view that teenagers are supposedly so hormone crazed that they need to have sex. But Christianity teaches that the act of sex is not just physical but spiritual and emotional. And because intimacy between two people is a reflection of the union between Christ (the man) and the church (the woman), people should abstain from sex until marriage.

Modern humanists would say that this standard imposes too much guilt on people and should therefore be eliminated. In a contemporary context, this "solution" has led to eliminating the prohibition against fornication, which has resulted in such highly questionable activities as handing out condoms after basketball games.

Communism provides us with yet another example of humanistic thinking. Communist ideology advances the idea that people are basically good, and yet Communism's greatest leaders—Lenin, Stalin, and Mao Zedong—carried out the most massive genocides in history. For being so basically "good," they certainly excelled at doing bad things.

By contrast, most of America's Founding Fathers believed that humans are basically sinful. This led to such concepts as the separation of church and state, justice dispensed by a jury made up of one's peers, impartial judges, an adversarial court system, the right of private citizens to bear arms, and many similar laws and rights that were designed to protect society and individual citizens from evil acts perpetrated by sinful people. All of these systems are in place so that we who are sinful can live in a good and just society.

The bottom line is that following the humanists' approach ultimately leaves us trapped in the destructive powers of sin. But the gospel offers us the power to live up to God's standard and *overcome* sin. The apostle Paul understood the evil hearts of people and our need for transformation. He also knew that even though the law maintains God's standard, it lacks the power to truly change us. When we have standards without power, we sin and are burdened with guilt. But when we appropriate God's power, we are able to live godly lives without guilt.

As crazy as it sounds, in too many churches today, the plan for upholding biblical standards is to eliminate or water down God's rules! That makes the ideas of humanists more the leader in these churches than Jesus.

In Christian circles we may have confused what the apostle Paul meant in his discussion about the difference between the Old Testament and New Testament approaches to God's law. Just like Jesus, Paul loved the law. He just knew that no one could perfectly obey it—so help was required. It was called *grace*. But grace did not cancel out God's standards for Christian behavior. Just because mercy and grace "trump" the law, we should not conclude that God's standards don't matter.

Does all of this have your head spinning? If so, don't feel alone! We live in a sea of confusion. Today the most basic truths are questioned, and what used to be considered wise is now supposedly foolish. The world has been turned upside down. What I'm discussing here is a very big deal because the result of casualness regarding standards encourages sin, and sin leads to tragedy and, ultimately, death of one kind or another. If the rules don't matter, husbands and wives can do whatever they want, a pastor can do whatever he wants, and a president can even do whatever he wants, because only a harsh, narrow-minded, evil, wicked person would say to others that they should be ashamed of their sinful behavior and live right by a particular set of standards.

Essentially what I am describing here is sloppy living, which influences small stuff, such as failing to keep a promise, not showing up on time, refusing to control your emotions, spending money unwisely, giving in to inappropriate sexual urges, getting drunk, driving too fast, dishonoring a parent—all kinds of foolishness. If you continue in this kind of sloppy living, people won't want to employ you, marry you, or share life with you, and it may affect your eternal destiny.

The New Testament has several of what I call "sloppy living" lists. I think it's helpful to review these sin lists so that we get a clear picture that it's not just "those sinners" out there who are guilty. We sinners "in here" are guilty of sin too. One sin list is found toward the end of Galatians:

> The acts of the sinful nature are obvious: sexual immorality, impurity and debauchery; idolatry and witchcraft; hatred, discord, jealousy, fits of rage, selfish ambition, dissensions, factions and envy; drunkenness, orgies, and the like. I warn you, as I did before, that those who live like this will not inherit the kingdom of God. (5:19-21)

Another list is in 1 Corinthians 6:9-10:

> Do you not know that the wicked will not inherit the kingdom of God? Do not be deceived: Neither the sexually immoral nor

idolaters nor adulterers nor male prostitutes nor homosexual offenders nor thieves nor the greedy nor drunkards nor slanderers nor swindlers will inherit the kingdom of God.

Another very interesting list in the book of Revelation reads:

But the cowardly, the unbelieving, the vile, the murderers, the sexually immoral, those who practice magic arts, the idolaters and all liars—their place will be in the fiery lake of burning sulfur. This is the second death. (21:8)

These lists define overt, more observable sinning, but then there are sins that might be called "couch potato" sins: thoughts and heart motivations that displease God, in addition to actions we know God wants us to take but we sit still, do nothing, and disobey.

You don't need a PhD from MIT to determine that we are all sinners and far more guilty than we realize or choose to admit. Sin is an enemy that will destroy us. This is all about spiritual survival. We are at war.

THE THREE BATTLEGROUNDS

The spiritual battle with sin is a three-front war.

The first battleground concerns the basic sin nature. Even if you've been a Christian since Truman was president, you will always be in combat on this sin front. This "you," or your *self*, wants always to have its way, but it must die. This is what the apostle Paul was talking about when he wrote,

We know that the law is spiritual; but I am unspiritual, sold as a slave to sin. I do not understand what I do. For what I want to do I do not do, but what I hate I do. And if I do what I do not want to do, I agree that the law is good. As it is, it is no longer I myself who do it, but it is sin living in me. I know that nothing good lives in me, that is, in my sinful nature. For I have the desire to do what is good, but I cannot carry it out. (Romans 7:14-18)

I wish it were not necessary, but I have the need to get up every morning and kill myself. I don't mean commit suicide—but I need to do what the Bible commands and die to myself. If I had not done this consistently throughout my Christian life, I would not be writing this book. I might not be a pastor. Who knows what I might be doing, because I must tell you, I definitely have a sin nature that consistently, repeatedly needs crushing. If I don't "kill myself" regularly, my sin nature slowly revives and resumes control. Hear me on this: At our core we are not good. *Nobody will ever become good through self-actualization.*

Right now it's in vogue to say, especially to young people, "You just need to be yourself. You need to discover yourself and let your true self out." Based on what I've just shared, can you imagine what awful, insane advice that is? Let me spare you much needless pain—if you are a parent, don't ever tell the three-year-old or the thirteen-year-old or the any-year-old in your family that! On our college campuses we are seeing all kinds of destructive behavior, from date rape to binge drinking. We should not be surprised at the results when we tell a self-centered, egotistical college student to "just find yourself and do what you want to do." What do we think will be the result with someone who does not know God and have the Holy Spirit in him or her?

The second sin battleground is with the devil and demons. We must recognize that we do have an adversary beyond ourselves. Because we all have an old sin nature and a tendency toward sin, there are times when forces of evil try to dominate our lives. Western theologians have gone to great lengths to explain that Christians cannot be *possessed* by evil spirits, but only oppressed. Though there is truth in this, it's unhelpful.

When the Bible addresses this subject, it doesn't differentiate between oppression and possession. Instead, it talks only about being *demonized,* which means "to be influenced by a demon or demons."

The goal is to remove the demonic influence and to be increasingly influenced by God's Word, God's Spirit, and God's people. The gospel provides the power for liberation. So if we will confront the powers of darkness and resist them, we will experience freedom and liberty in Christ.

The third front in the battle against sin is the area of sowing and reaping—the flesh and the spirit. If you sow to the flesh, you'll reap out of the flesh; if you sow to the spirit, you'll reap out of the spirit. It's basic truth. If you invest yourself in the things of the world, your dividends will be worldly. This means that if you watch movies or TV shows that glamorize immoral behavior, don't be shocked if you start having lustful thoughts and find yourself losing the battle to stay moral.

Fortunately, the sowing and reaping principle works for the good, too. If you fill your eyes and mind with images and ideas that emphasize the ways of God, you will become more godly. If you meditate on the Word of God, you'll have the ammunition you need to fight off temptation.

The good news is there's a treatment to cure sin. We must not capitulate to contemporary humanistic ideas and remove the standard, kidding ourselves by insisting that men and women are basically good. The truth is, we all are basically bad and need standards. The way we can stop being bad and become good is to let Jesus save us and then give us the power of His Holy Spirit to live by God's standards.

The solution to the problems caused by the "s" word is the gospel. In the next chapter we will look at why the good news is really *fantastic* news.

Questions for Pastor Ted

I hear the teaching on how to let go of the old sin nature, but I struggle with letting go. I keep holding on to the sins and mistakes of the past. What can I do to really let go?

Everyone has this struggle. You are not alone. First, I'd encourage you to read some books that explain how to forgive yourself. (*Forgive and Forget* by Lewis Smedes is a good place to start.) Be honest with yourself and God about your struggle to let go of the past. Open your heart to receive His love and forgiveness. Then, begin to pray about the future. Press ahead and let God create a wonderful new future for you. Don't spend your time thinking about what might have been if the past had been different. Learn the lessons from the past, forgive those who were involved—including yourself—then take the wisdom from those experiences and move toward the future God has planned for you (see Philippians 3:12-14).

What do you think when someone says, "The devil made me do it"?

I think it's a cop-out. It's just an excuse people use in an attempt to explain the difference between their noble desires and the corrupt reality of their actions.

Christians, especially, should understand that Satan is a defeated foe. In Genesis 3:14 God said to the serpent, "Because you have done this, cursed are you above all the livestock and all the wild animals! You will crawl on your belly and you will eat dust all the days of your life." Simply put, Satan is lower than a cockroach. He doesn't even have the authority of a mosquito! The difference is that mosquitoes and cockroaches can't whisper to people and influence their thoughts and emotions like the Enemy can. The fact that the devil and his demons can whisper and are intelligent and sinister makes them worthy—but defeated—foes. Satan attempts to trigger our old sin nature and cause us to think and act contrary to God's plan.

Romans 8:12 says, "Therefore, brothers, we have an obligation—but it is not to the sinful nature, to live according to it." The bottom line here is that as followers of Christ, we have been set free from the bondage of our old sin nature. We need not fear the Enemy, but instead we may exercise the authority over him that God has given us.

It is clear in 1 John 3:8 that "the reason the Son of God appeared was to destroy the devil's work"—and He did just that on the cross. So when people sin, they should take personal responsibility for it. The devil can't *make* people do anything without their cooperation. And why would anyone want to cooperate with something lower than a cockroach?

No more excuses. We're filled with the Holy Spirit and have a life-giving body of believers around us for support. We might as well live in victory!

Four

GRACE TO YOU

I know God loves me. I know God gave His Son for me. I know Jesus died on the cross for me. I also know that some people who love me might not like me if they knew the dark side of me, the side that doubts and struggles.

Hmm. God loves me, but does He *like* me? I love God, but do I *like* Him? What about you?

Regardless of your answer, by the time you finish this chapter, I want you to receive a fresh revelation of God's feelings and actions toward us.

You may be thinking, *Oh, this is a fortunate development! Since I already know I'm a believer, I'll just save some time and jump ahead to chapter 5.*

No, no! Don't do that! To show you why I say this, let me ask you a few questions. (Relax, this is not a test—you will not be graded!)

- Do you think you don't read your Bible enough?
- Do you think you don't pray enough?
- Do you think your mind isn't as clean as it should be?
- Do you think you don't give enough?
- Do you think you don't volunteer enough to teach Sunday school or work in the nursery at church?

Well, let me take a load off your mind. Jesus died on the cross to cover stuff like that. Jesus died for our lack of Bible reading and prayer, for our failures, our bad thought life—every area in which we fall short. (Except, perhaps, for not working in the nursery!) Because of the blood the Lord Jesus Christ shed on the cross, we are acceptable to God.

In my experience, too many people have never truly experienced grace—never been overwhelmed by the indescribable enormity of God's love. Part of the problem may be that we need encounters with grace every day, not just at the moment we receive salvation. We live among people who are crying out for grace. Marriages are broken, millions of girls and boys are fatherless, covenants between people are casually discarded, employers betray employees and employees betray employers. Too many church leaders have lied to their sheep, and congregations are a wreck. All of this human, hurting mess needs the grace of God.

So as you begin to read this chapter, I want you to stop what you are doing and ask God to astound you with the truth of how much grace He has for you—how limitless is His love and care.

If you don't normally have intimate conversations with God, find a place where you can be alone and just talk to Him. And let Him get a word in too—don't you do all the talking. Just pray something like this,

> Lord God, I ask now that through the ministry of the
> Holy Spirit, the love of Jesus would be shown to me. I pre-
> sent my heart to You. Parts of my heart are hard. I've been
> betrayed and hurt. God, I want You to soften my heart so
> that my spirit will be open to You and Your life will be made

real in me. Lord, I open myself to You now. Please come
and meet with me. I love You and want to spend time connecting with You. Wash me clean with the blood of Jesus.
Fill me up with Your Spirit. Open my spiritual ears so I can
hear what You want to say to me. Heal my wounds and
remove every barrier between us. Today I want to appropriate—to receive—in a new way an understanding of the love
of Jesus and the grace of God. I trust You for that, in Jesus's
name. Amen.

THE WORK OF GOD

We do not get very far into the book of Galatians before we see Paul
expressing amazement that his converts and friends are already confused about grace:

> I am astonished that you are so quickly deserting the one who
> called you by the grace of Christ and are turning to a different
> gospel—which is really no gospel at all. Evidently some people
> are throwing you into confusion and are trying to pervert the
> gospel of Christ. (1:6-7)

Paul was beside himself! How could any sane person turn away
from the true gospel or "good news"? And I must emphasize, it is
really good news. Jesus came to set you free, not to make you sad and
sorry. He came to give you power, not a new expanded version of rules
and regulations.

A major purpose Paul had in writing this letter was to remind the
members of the Galatian church that salvation is by grace alone.

The body of Christ today is well structured, financed, administered, and housed, but I don't think we are all that great at loving one another freely, joyfully, expansively. This may be so because people don't understand the grace of God and are in some sense trying to work for their salvation. Or maybe it's because people have been wounded and have allowed their hearts to turn bitter. Whatever the reason, it's tragic because we have been created to love God and one another. My fear is that we'll live our lives never truly opening ourselves up to receive God's love and, as a result, never truly loving others. We need to be overcome, consumed, strengthened, and, ultimately, empowered by God's love.

That's what grace is all about.

The Meaning of Grace

Many keywords are required to adequately define grace. To start, though, I must confess that the popular, well-accepted definition of *grace*—"God's unmerited favor"—contains one word I don't like. That statement certainly is true—we don't deserve God's favor, but the word *unmerited* really does some disservice to the rich meaning of grace. I think it might be better to just use the word *favor* and drop the unmerited part. Here's why.

Too often when grace is explained as "unmerited favor," the emphasis lands more on "unmerited" than on "favor." So the message that sticks is, "Yes, you're saved by the grace of God, but you know that it's *unmerited* because you're so worthless. You're just a dog! You're a bad person. You're evil. You're wicked. Don't get too happy. God will save you by His grace, but be thankful because you just made it by the skin of your teeth!"

So, surprise, surprise, we often don't get too excited about this message. That's one of the reasons I want you to think about this and, after thinking and praying, open yourself to receive a deeper revelation of God's grace. Too many of us say we understand and appreciate grace, but in our hearts we have a kind of "whatever" reaction. We don't feel much confidence because we sense we are dangling over the pit of hell. After all, we know too well what's going on inside us. That word *unmerited* is clanging like a loud bell, drowning out the affirmations of love that God is whispering in our ears. We think that if we are fortunate, we'll catch God in a good mood and escape the punishment we truly deserve. *By the grace of God,* we'll get saved and make it to heaven somehow.

My friend, that's not the grace I'm talking about! I don't believe that's what the Word teaches either. If Paul heard you talk like that, he would write you a letter—actually, an e-mail—and he would soundly scorch you. Too many of us are dragging around with a frown on our hearts when we should be dancing and rejoicing and walking in confidence with God—enjoying our prayer times, interceding for others, operating in the power of the Spirit, growing in the wonderful life of God.

Do you relate to any of this? Do you think that God just tolerates you, but if He sees you coming into Starbucks, all of a sudden He packs up His laptop, averts His eyes, and hurries out the door?

Do I have *good news* for you!

God is sold on you. He wants you free. He wants you filled with His Spirit. He wants you healed. He wants you strong. He wants you empowered. I'm talking about *you!*

God will not deny you. He will not reject you. He will not turn His back on you and run away. He is waiting for you. And what's even more cool, He not only loves you, He *likes* you. He enjoys hanging out with you. He likes your hair and what you're wearing today. He likes your glasses. He thinks you're lovable. He's your adoring Daddy.

I know you may be saying, "That's all well and good for you, Ted, but you don't know me. You don't know what I've done. You don't know what I was thinking just a minute ago." No, I don't know you. But I know God and what He has promised. Grace was His idea. So get over yourself! Jesus is for you, whether you like it and feel it or not. Jesus admires you. Jesus went up on a cross for you. You were planned before the creation of the world to be alive right now. He knows what your inner problems are. He knows it all, and He enjoys you with everything He's got—His very life.

Here's another Haggardism: *There's nobody who knows your sin life like Jesus, and He's still sold on you.*

When God revealed to me what He really meant by grace, it changed me—the way I walk, the things I buy, the tone of my voice, the places I go, and the way I treat my wife, our children, and other people. Everything. I felt like the happiest, most grateful person on earth. I think Paul felt this way too, and that is what he wanted the Galatian believers to experience. He did not want them to be robbed of the grace he had taught them about.

GRACE TO YOU

A definition of grace that I prefer is this: Grace is God's favor that transforms our hearts and changes our actions.

So if you say, "I am free from sin by the grace of God," that means God touched your heart, which changed your actions. As a result, you are not a slave to sin anymore. Or if you say, "The power of God's grace has changed me," it means God's influence upon your heart and its reflection in your life has caused you to stop doing the harmful things you did in the past. No one doubts God's ability to change lives. Why does He change our lives? Because He favors us. He likes us. He wants to give us many wonderful blessings. He has our best in mind. That's His grace. But to misunderstand grace and use it as a license for disobedience rather than a truth to appropriate obedience is a significant distortion of the intent of God.

In addition to favor, the concept of "pleasure" is also strongly evident in the meaning of grace. That may sound weird, but God draws pleasure from us. I learned this firsthand years ago when I was still a college kid.

A group of us was traveling the country, doing a summer music-ministry tour. (Believe me, I was there to preach, not to sing!) We had stopped at a church where the senior pastor was a great big—I mean really tall and heavy—man. One day he did a nice thing for us and said, "Ted, I understand you like to water-ski. We have made arrangements to get a speedboat and skis. You all go have a great time."

I thanked the pastor and said, "Hey, why don't you come with us?" But honestly, as I said it I was thinking, *Man, this guy's so big he's going to bog down the whole boat.* But with a little more coaxing, he finally agreed to come along.

We went to the lake and started taking turns skiing and messing around—except for the pastor, who stayed in the boat. It was super fun. We were doing flips and turns, even trying a little barefoot action. Next we decided to hook up a rubber mat and do tricks on it. The only way to do this right is to crank up the boat to high speed so the water is firm and you can get up on the mat.

We were taking turns performing—like putting the ski rope in our mouths and doing "Look, Mom, no hands!" and that kind of thing. As we were racing around, I started thinking that we needed to get our pastor friend in the water riding that mat. He was the nicest guy, but, in my opinion, he was taking life way too seriously. Every time I was in the boat, he wanted to discuss theology. There we were, flying over the water—the wind and outboard motor howling—and he was shouting at me, "Ted, what do you think about what John Wesley said about such and such?" Something had to be done.

"Hey, Pastor, why don't you take a ride on the mat?" He wouldn't hear of it at first and just wanted to get back to our theological discussion. But finally I convinced him. He jumped into the water, which made the boat float higher in the water by several inches. I showed him how to reach up over his head, wrap his arms around the mat behind him, and lay on the mat face up. Then I explained how he needed to respond when we got up to speed so he wouldn't submarine and drink half the lake.

Finally we were ready. I yelled out, "This will be easy, Pastor. Just hold on no matter what!"

If you've never done this, I need to explain that when you're on a mat like that, you take off, and it drags in the water until you get enough speed and the mat "planes"—rises more on top of the surface so there is a smooth ride without too much spray. Once the mat planes, you can do tricks and enjoy the ride, skimming across the top of the water. The heavier you are, the faster the boat has to go to get the mat to plane out.

I knew that this would be a challenge because of the pastor's size, so I moved all the other riders to the front of the boat. When the pastor was set and everyone was ready, I opened up the throttle all the way. The prow rose up and we pulled away—the boat motor roaring—but we could not get the pastor and his mat to plane. Instead of having a smooth, fun ride, he plowed through the water, a huge bubble shooting up around him, and water rippling down his back—tickling him. So there he was—his flesh wiggling and jiggling, the water cascading up over his head and down his back and giving him the tickle of his life.

What we saw and heard behind us was this wall of spray with two little hands sticking out the front and a roar of laughter and occasional yells, "Ha ha ha ha ha ha—ah—ha ha ha ha ha ha—ah—ha ha ha ha ha ha—Stop, can't breathe!—ah—ha ha ha ha ha ha!"

We never did get the pastor's mat to plane, but we all had a great time. And, for sure, it ended the pastor's questions on topics like eternal security and the end times.

But the big shocker for me was this: In the middle of the pastor's water frolic, the Holy Spirit came on me and gave me an insight on grace. Really! (Does that happen to you, too? The Spirit whispers something really great when you least expect it?) While the pastor was laughing as he plowed through the water, the Holy Spirit said to me, *I'm enjoying that guy right now more than I have in fifteen years!*

I was awestruck. I told the other team members about it later, and they said, "Haggard, you're hearing too many voices. This is getting really strange!"

Yes, it was kind of strange, but it gave me an insight into God's tender, benevolent affection for His children and impressed on me how I wanted to live my life. I realized that God delights in us and gains much pleasure from just watching us live our lives. After that day I never wanted to do anything but give God pleasure. I wanted it to be true that every time God looked on the earth—with all the poverty, all the abuse, all the despair, all the hurt, all the things that would sadden and break His heart—when He came to me and gave a look, He would smile and laugh—with me, of course, not at me! I wanted God to get a kick out of me.

I thank that dear, big-brother pastor for helping me learn that when the apostle Paul or others wrote, "Grace to you," it meant "May the pleasure of God be strong in you—the ability to grow in Him, please Him, bring honor to Him, be enjoyed by Him, and maybe even make Him laugh."

Nobody loves you like God loves you. Nobody admires you the way He admires you. No one is more sold on the value of your life than God. No one thinks you have more intrinsic worth than He does.

God looks at you as a Father looks at his son playing baseball. God sees you as a Father sees his daughter at her first gymnastics meet. God says, "Did you see him hit that home run? That's My boy! Did you see her do that flip? That's My girl!"

Do you know someone who brings a smile to your face when you see him coming? You want to spend time with him. You enjoy being with him. You're never nervous about what to talk about with him because you like each other. You get a kick out of each other, even when you know the worst things about each other. You see this person through eyes of love, not scrutiny—just as God looks at you.

Another keyword that describes grace is "benefit." If you are a mom or dad, you know the joy of bestowing benefits upon or "gracing" your children. And as a parent, the more you have, the more you are able to give your kids. Some kids receive more benefits from their parents than other kids receive from theirs. Well, God is no different, and He has a *lot* to bestow. He's not mean, and He doesn't withhold things from us out of spite. He's not stingy. He's not worried about running out. He loves giving.

Here are some benefits God wants to grace you with: He wants to surround you with angels, protect you, respond to you, deliver you, heal you, justify you, sanctify you. He wants to cleanse you, renew you, empower you, strengthen you. He wants to pour His Spirit into you. He'll give you everything He has. He'll give you His name, His nature, His Word. He'll give you His will—and the power to fulfill it. He'll give you absolutely everything He has. He'll come off His own throne and do it for you Himself. If you ever say, "I don't know if I can do it," remember, Jesus has already done it all for you, and He sent His Spirit to help you.

Rest in the loving arms of God. He wants to benefit you.

Related to God's benefits are His gifts. He wants to give you miracles and amazing abilities—the gifts of the Holy Spirit. He gives liberally. With Him there's no shortage of love, peace, caring, and kindness.

A final word that helps reveal God's grace is *gratitude*.

Here in Colorado Springs we have a Schwan's man who goes door to door selling ice cream and other products. During the summer I look forward to the arrival of the Schwan's truck, so we can buy fudgies, mud pie ice-cream sandwiches, orange-sherbet push-ups, and strawberry fruit bars. What makes buying these treats wonderful is the fact that I love my children. I love giving them things that make them happy, and I can keep giving them an abundance of these things as long as they are grateful as well.

This is the way God's grace is. He loves it when we obey, when we respond, when we seek Him, when we joyfully give, serve, love, and grow. If we whine, complain, and excessively contemplate, I think it bores Him. But when we are grateful, responsive servants of God, He is able to enjoy His benevolence toward us.

Grace results in a beautiful relationship. God favors you, is grateful for you, draws pleasure from you, appreciates you, accepts you, loves filling you with His Spirit, wants to empower you to make your life valuable to others. He loves meeting with you, gets a kick out of you, enjoys you, laughs with you. It's love. It's admiration. It's affection. It's pleasure. It's enjoyment.

The one word for all of this is *grace!*

Grace empowers, strengthens, transforms, renews. Grace gives us the power to obey and walk in victory. It gives us the freedom to live better lives. Grace also empowers us to trust God and persevere when we face difficulties.

Paul once mentioned that the riches of God's grace were "incomparable" (Ephesians 2:7). That makes me want to shout "Hallelujah!" and then gratefully fall to my knees in awe.

So what do you think? Do you have a richer understanding of God's grace after reading this chapter?

We started with a prayer; let's end it that way too:

Dear Father, oh my, thank You, thank You, thank You for
Your grace. It makes all the difference to me. How could I live
without Your grace in my life? I receive joyfully in my heart
this new revelation of Your favor toward me. Fill me with the
Holy Spirit. I boldly lay claim to Your grace and the fresh life
Jesus wants for me. I want it all, God—every good and perfect
gift You so graciously bestow. Thank You for Your love, Your
favor, Your benefits, Your gifts—Your grace. In Jesus's name, I
pray. Amen.

Questions for Pastor Ted

You mention the well-accepted definition of grace as "God's unmerited favor" but say that the word unmerited "does some disservice to the rich meaning of grace." Could you talk about this a bit more?

God gives us blessings and cares for us as a voluntary gesture from His heart. We don't earn His favor; it's a free gift. But too often when we talk about God's favor, we get the idea that we are worthless. That's not true. The value of an item is assessed by its purchase price. God didn't purchase us with silver or gold. We couldn't be purchased with any amount of money. God purchased us with the life of Jesus, His Son. That is our worth to Him. He values us. So when "unmerited" is overemphasized, it actually changes the meaning of grace.

I think it's valuable to teach that God's gifts are available based on His merit, not our own. But at the same time, God decided we were worth purchasing. This needs to be clear, or we will misunderstand the relationship God wants to have with us.

Why is it hard for us to believe that God delights in our joy?

Because so much of religious practice is way too serious and introspective. Since Jesus has provided so much for every one of us, we have great cause for delight. Certainly, meditation is important. Meditating on Scripture is the way to discover a deep core of joy that no situation or human being can take away from us. Religious folks have always pushed joyless contemplation. Fortunately, that's not the gospel.

Heaven will be fun, exciting, and holy. There is a time to be awed by His majesty, and there is a time to rejoice. In both there is great joy. Smile!

A DIFFERENT GOSPEL?

W hy would anyone want a "different" gospel?

This was the question that so confounded the apostle Paul two thousand years ago. It's a question that still bewilders us today. Why would anyone not eagerly, joyfully embrace the grace offered through the gospel of the Lord Jesus? What else is worth even considering?

Let's look again at the verses where Paul expressed his confusion on the issue to the Galatians:

> I am astonished that you are so quickly deserting the one who
> called you by the grace of Christ and are turning to a different
> gospel—which is really no gospel at all. Evidently some people
> are throwing you into confusion and are trying to pervert the
> gospel of Christ. (1:6-7)

Why did Paul use such strong language to criticize the Galatians for their messing around with the meaning of the gospel? When Paul wrote that they were turning to a "different gospel," he wasn't saying that they were splitting hairs over some doctrinal issue, like perhaps a difference over a "nonessential" that might divide a Baptist from a

Nazarene. No, what Paul was accusing them of was heading off in a whole new direction.

In our time, for example, it would be more like the differences that exist between Mormons and evangelical Christians. The Mormons construct buildings that look like traditional churches, and they appear to have a mainstream Christian message. They'll say, "Oh, yes, we believe in Jesus, and we believe in the Bible as you do." But it's not true. They have a different gospel that does not communicate salvation by grace through faith.

You might be thinking, *Isn't this stuff on Mormons pretty narrow thinking? Is Ted some kind of religious bigot?* If you think I'm tough, check out how the apostle Paul responded to those who were twisting the truth in Galatia. He was so impassioned you can almost see the smoke rising from the scribe's quill.

> But even if we [meaning Barnabas, Titus, and Paul] or
> an angel from heaven should preach a gospel other
> than the one we preached to you, let him be eternally
> condemned! (verse 8)

This is amazing! Paul didn't write that if a demon or an angel says this, then you should reject the message. No, Paul made it clear that if even the most reliable authority—himself or an angel from *heaven*—should deliver such a different message, he should be eternally condemned.

If Muhammed supposedly heard a different gospel from Allah or a guy named Joseph Smith walked out of the woods with some stone tablets with a different message, "don't buy into it." According to

Paul, anyone who does this is accursed and in danger of eternal condemnation. He insists that the gospel message is more important than any messenger, culture, old idea, new theory, majority opinion, personal preference—anything. The gospel is the absolute core of God's plan for all people in all ages. It must not be changed or compromised in any way.

When he said this, Paul was not having a bad day or using hyperbole to make a point. He wasn't exaggerating to get people's attention or trying to create some buzz. Obviously Paul had not been to his editor to find out how to word this so it wouldn't offend anybody, nor had he hired a publicist to get the spin and talking points just right. Forget that. Paul meant exactly what he said.

The Greek word he used here that gives us the English words "eternally condemned" is *anathema,* which means "accursed and damned." It conveys the idea of going to hell. The word *anathema* does not imply that if somebody starts spreading a different gospel, it's a minor mistake and God will give a spanking and then follow it up with a hug. It's true that God is a kind, loving Father and disciplines in the best interests of His children. But the word Paul used here does not describe that quality of God's personality. *Anathema* reveals God as a righteous judge who is saying, "You've been found guilty! The sentence for this is death with no opportunity for appeal."

Paul said this so harshly because he knew how serious God is about the truth. Paul had to be tough and warn the Galatians—and us, too—that misrepresenting the gospel is a hugely important matter with God.

Some preachers today would propose that Paul must have been confused—that there's no way the God we know now could be so disapproving, so intolerant. That strikes me as a dangerous idea to promote. Paul wrote what he wrote. He meant it when he said that to advocate some variation of God's truth is to put yourself opposite of God's grace, to flirt with condemnation. To mess with the gospel is to mess with God.

But even the fiery Paul knew that he was getting himself in trouble by using such strong language. So he wrote next, "Am I now trying to win the approval of men, or of God? Or am I trying to please men?" (verse 10).

He knew people were going to say, "Paul, you are a narrowly focused, bigoted, intolerant, unkind, high-minded jerk. How in the world could you really believe that God is so strict and that there is only one way to eternal life? What do you mean that other people are going to go to hell? Oh, how horrible you are!"

So the apostle Paul continued, "If I were still trying to please men, I would not be a servant of Christ" (verse 10).

Brilliant! Paul cleverly made his point. Then he went on to explain how he received his revelation of truth:

> I want you to know, brothers, that the gospel I preached is
> not something that man made up. I did not receive it from
> any man, nor was I taught it; rather, I received it by revelation
> from Jesus Christ. (verses 11-12)

In other words, Paul said, "I know the truth. I received it from the Source of truth."

Paul was so devoted to the truth of the gospel that he was willing to take on anyone, even the apostle Peter. Indeed, they had a tense conflict. It happened in the great city of Antioch, where the term *Christian* was coined. Paul ministered there and was much loved. The believers in Antioch had a custom of gathering together to eat and enjoy fellowship. We can imagine the setting. Both Jewish and Gentile followers of Jesus were eating, laughing, and sharing with one another.

We still do this kind of thing in our churches today. It doesn't matter if you are older or younger, or if you come from an influential, well-to-do family or one that's barely holding itself together; everybody just eats together and enjoys the fellowship.

Peter had come to Antioch for a visit and was attending these potlucks. Like everyone else, he was enjoying himself thoroughly. But when some men came from the church in Jerusalem, Peter separated himself from the Gentile believers because he was afraid of these men from the circumcision group. The other Jews, including Barnabas, joined him in this hypocrisy.

We might have thought that by now Peter would have seen through the problem behind this separating of Jewish and Gentile believers. But he caved in, and this really bugged Paul. So he took Peter on:

> When I saw that they were not acting in line with the truth of
> the gospel, I said to Peter in front of them all, "You are a Jew,
> yet you live like a Gentile and not like a Jew. How is it, then,
> that you force Gentiles to follow Jewish customs?" (2:14)

In effect, he said to Peter, "Hold on! What are you doing separating yourself as a Jewish man from these Gentile brothers and sisters in Christ? You can't do that! It's wrong. It's contrary to the whole idea of the gospel!" And, of course, in time Peter ended up agreeing with Paul.

The way Paul confronted Peter is a great example of how we can all guard against deception. Peter believed something that was reasonable, thoughtful, persuasive, logical, and *wrong*. It was a denial of the basic premise of the gospel. Here he was, a disciple, a close friend of Jesus, an influential leader in the church. But he was blind—deceived.

Another Haggardism: *The problem with deception is that it's so incredibly deceiving!*

We don't even know when we've been deceived. A deceived person will never say, "You know, I'm deceived about such and such." A deceived person cannot say that; it would be contrary to the definition of the word.

Normally, deception is revealed only when a good friend comes up and says something like, "Shape up! Stop treating your wife that way. Don't talk to your kids like that. How in the world can you believe that nonsense?"

Now if we respond arrogantly to this kind of honest input, we deserve to be called foolish. But if we respond humbly, saying, "Thanks! I trust you as a good friend. Help me think this through. Help me see it. Help me work it out," then we will come out of the deceptive fog and start seeing the truth.

We should not unfairly criticize Peter. Responses like his have occurred repeatedly in Christendom down through the ages. In our day some people call themselves Christians but are actually racists. That's wrong. We need to confront such insults to the gospel and say,

"You are denying the gospel message of the Lord Jesus Christ by being a racist! You must love all people the way God loves all people."

NOTHING BUT THE TRUTH

Paul was very confident that he knew the truth. You may say, "That's great for him, but I struggle with keeping clear what is both true and important."

The conflict between Paul and Peter does remind us of how Christians often still disagree about things. (Now that's an understatement that should qualify me for some kind of award!) How are we to know when to stand and fight for something or when it might be a good idea to just smile, nod our heads, and go get another doughnut?

There are some core, foundational truths that the church has believed for two thousand years, and they continue to be true regardless of the society in which one lives—be it pluralistic or traditional, free market or socialist. Whether we live in a democracy or under a dictator's thumb, these truths remain constant and absolute. They are essentials of the faith and not open for debate.

A number of other ideas are important and bring great insight and benefit to all of us. But they are not absolutes, and they are open for debate. The question is, "How do you tell the difference?"

On the following page is a simple illustration I developed some years ago that I believe will help us find the answer to this question. I call it Ted's Truth Target.

At the center of the target—the bull's-eye—are the core *absolutes*. These are the nonnegotiable truths of our faith that all orthodox Christians in the past, present, and future embrace. Some examples would be:

- the deity of Christ and His Virgin Birth
- the full inspiration and authority of the Bible, which is God's Word
- the inherent corruption of the human race—otherwise known as original sin
- the utter "lostness" of humanity without the shed blood of Christ
- salvation by grace through faith in Christ as Savior and Lord

Such absolute truths are worth getting a bloody nose over. You should not be involved in any church or ministry that ignores or

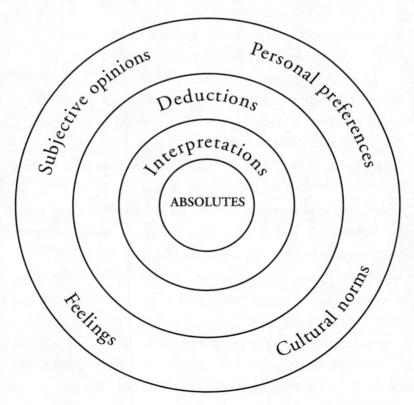

twists these essentials. Absolutes tend to be stated straightforwardly in Scripture.

The next ring on our truth target is *interpretations*. These are often mistaken as absolutes. One way to evaluate whether a particular teaching is an essential or an interpretation is to observe carefully how the idea is discussed. An essential is often just read out of the Bible. An interpretation often comes after a Bible passage is read, and a speaker says these key words: "Let me tell you what this means." In other words, interpretations are, uh, interpretations. Certainly, many interpretations are good-as-gold truth. But they still have as their foundation the understanding and explanations of human interpreters.

An example of an interpretation would be Communion—just exactly what does happen when the elements are taken? Do they become the *actual* body and blood of Jesus, or are they just symbolic representations of His body and blood? You could argue that one until Jesus comes again, which brings me to another example of an interpretation: the various ideas about the end times. *Don't get me started!* Well, I started myself. Some guy will stand and say that the number seven in the book of Daniel or Revelation means this and three means this and a thousand means this and a day means this many years and—*presto!*—this is how we know when Jesus will come. *Hello!* I would say that proves the guy has too much time on his hands and is in over his head in interpretations. (But he might write a book and sell boatloads more than I ever would. Am I envious? Does it show?)

Good, godly, righteous, sincere brothers and sisters in Christ come up with very different interpretations of what Scripture teaches on a multitude of subjects. Just remember that interpretations are not absolutes; I don't believe anyone will gain or lose salvation based on interpretations. However, the ultimate destiny of people is affected by their response to absolutes.

Although many noses are bloodied, get bent out of joint, and are even broken in conflicts over interpretations, I do not think they are worth fighting over. However, if someone were to say that he or she is a Christian and then insist that Jesus's death on the cross did not provide atonement for our sins, he or she would be attacking an absolute, and that's worthy of throwing some punches (figuratively speaking!). But if someone insists that "three verses read backward in the book of Daniel prove without a doubt that Jesus visited North America and established the area now known as California as the Promised Land," nod knowingly, excuse yourself, and go get another doughnut.

The third ring from the center of the bull's-eye is what I describe as *deductions*. A deduction typically occurs when you take one portion of Scripture, add it to one (or more) other passages of Scripture, and arrive at a certain conclusion or deduction. This is the classic A + B = C approach, with C being the deduction. Deductions often occur in discussions of end-times prophecy. A person will say, "In Daniel it says such and such, and in Revelation it says so-and-so; therefore, we conclude that Jesus's return will look like this." That's a deduction, which means the odds that it's wrong are quite high.

Deductions may be frivolous, such as the statement that all dogs or horses go to heaven. Actually, I've played around with my own deduction and propose that dogs and horses—as opposed to cats—probably do go to heaven. Here's my reasoning: Dogs are basically nice, devoted pets that respond well to the authority of their owners. It's less true with horses, but maybe if they were smaller and we could have them as house pets, they would also be more gracious. The big evidence for horses in heaven is that Jesus has chosen to ride a horse when He returns!

If this sounds silly, I am successfully making my point about the often questionable validity of deductions!

Now, cats—I have serious issues with cats. Actually, I think I can make something approaching an absolute statement about cats: Without a doubt, they will all go to hell! Before you send me an e-mail, let me explain. It's just a matter of constructing an ironclad deduction. Every cat I've ever known was arrogant, high-minded, and definitely not submissive. Cats just don't have much time for authority. Have you ever tried to teach a cat to do tricks? Good luck! A cat eats when it wants to eat, drinks when it wants to drink, and so on. It is entirely given over to self-will. In the Bible there's no record of a cat even getting the crumbs under the table—unlike the dog referred to by the Canaanite woman. Cats won't be in heaven. I'm convinced.

Okay, I'm being funny—or trying to be funny. Please don't send me a picture of your cat answering the telephone. *I'm only kidding.* I have met a few cats I kind of liked. I'm just not planning to take them with me. But I don't want any of my dogs in heaven, either, shedding hair throughout the mansion! I *really don't know* whether animals will be in heaven. I'm just making a point.

One of my special Haggardisms: *Be careful about betting the farm on favorite deductions.*

My hunch is that when all is said and done—after Jesus arrives on His horse—we will find out that most deductions were wrong, as were many interpretations. I recommend sticking with absolutes and holding on lightly to all the rest—except for doughnuts; keep a firm grip on those, especially when dogs are in the room!

Oh my, you can see there are still more categories on the perimeter of Ted's Truth Target. We Christians are loaded with *subjective opinions*. These are expressed when people say, "Well, I have an opinion about this or that. I like this, and I don't like that." Often these opinions have no connection to Scripture.

Here's an example of one of my own beloved subjective opinions: *I really dislike church pews*. I'm a guy who likes my space. Sure, I am all for brotherly-sisterly love and think the body of Christ is totally cool. But does that mean I have to sit squished between Frank and Irma on Sunday morning? I don't think so. I love them, but give me my space. I don't want strangers rubbing against me. In my opinion, the way to go is to have comfortable chairs in a church—complete with those little armrests in between seats.

In our congregation, when we were getting ready to build a new sanctuary, a group approached me with the idea that the new seating should be pews. I said, "Off with their heads!" No, I didn't say *that!* We do have nice soft chairs with rigid metal armrests between them all, however.

I admit that my pew phobia is nothing more than a subjective opinion. You won't get any argument from me. Heaven will be full of people who sat on pews. If you want a big mess in a church, though, start confusing subjective opinions with absolutes. You will need a quart jar of aspirin to numb all the headaches. Subjective opinions are just personal preferences. Some people like blue carpet; others like red. Some people like hymns; others like choruses. Subjective opinions are neither godly nor ungodly. They're just personal preferences and must be recognized for what they are.

Cultural norms can also confuse us. They can seem very important because most of us like security—and there's a lot of comfort in doing things the way "they've always been done where we're from." Should the pastor wear a robe, or is it okay if he wears jeans and a sweatshirt? Should the podium be in the center of the platform, or is any podium a sign of dead tradition? Drums or organ? Should the church building look like Westminster Abbey or a supersized Wal-Mart? All such questions relate to cultural norms. Again, keep the aspirin close by if you devote yourself to too many discussions of such issues. Nobody can really say he or she is right about such things, but that won't prevent an argument. Take two aspirin and go get another doughnut.

If you haven't guessed it by now, my tongue is cemented to my cheek. And for my final foray into the sacred-that-isn't-really-all-that-sacred, I give you the most important thing in all of life for the church community: *feelings*. Way too many church decisions are based on such questions as, "How does the place make you feel?" "Are you comfortable or not?" "Do shivers run down your spine during wor-ship—or was that a hot flash?" "Does the pastor's sermon make your heart beat fast, or is it heartburn?" Barry Manilow may have unknow-ingly recorded the church's greatest praise song: "Feelings"!

We don't even ask people what they think anymore. We just ask, "How do you *feel* about it?" Because how we feel about something is so much more important than what we *think* about it or what we *know* about it. Feelings too often supersede facts.

I encourage you to make a list of core absolutes—the truths you can build your faith and life upon. Then use my little chart to keep all of the other ideas and traditions in perspective.

As Paul so capably and ardently argued, there is only one gospel.

It's true. It's not different and won't change. Leave it alone. It's well worth fighting for. All of the rest of the stuff makes for interesting discussions.

Just keep the doughnuts handy!

Questions for Pastor Ted

If someone you know is very strong in his or her opinion about something you think is a deduction or an interpretation of Scripture, is it best to just back out of the conversation? In other words, should we just eat a dough-nut and move on? Or should we take time to explain the difference between an absolute, a deduction, and an interpretation in an effort to help the person realize that this isn't something worth stirring up division?

I think it depends upon the depth of your relationship with the person. If you don't have much of a relationship, and he or she lectures you on some topic that doesn't really matter, let it go. But if this person asks your opinion, answer the question by explaining the difference between absolutes, deductions, interpretations, and so on. Whether you agree or disagree on the matter at hand, the person needs to know that his or her position is not an absolute. If the person doesn't understand this, someone somewhere sometime might really embarrass him or her.

We all feel strongly about some interpretations and deductions, and we think highly of our cultural norms and preferences. If we want to emphasize some of these ideas even though they are a long way from the absolutes, that's okay. And having strong convictions about our preferences is fine as well. But when we express our views, we need to do so "with gentleness and respect" (1 Peter 3:15), and we need to make sure we don't insist that others accept our preferences—including our "revelations" from God—as "absolutes."

I once spoke to a woman who was best friends with a married man, and she did not see the danger in this situation. She was someone who prayed every day, studied her Bible, and tried to be a doer of the Word. No matter how much I talked to her about it, she kept saying, "God told me He gave me this person as a friend." When people seem to be truly seeking after God but then turn in some crazy direction or make unwise choices, are they being deceived or foolish?

Maybe both. The solution to this, though, is connecting with other believers in a positive way. The reason God places us in families and in local churches is so that we will have people in our lives to help us see our blind spots. This woman would have been wise to trust you instead of saying, "God told me to do this." The vast majority of people are the cause of their own heartaches, and they need to listen to the wisdom of godly people around them. This woman certainly needs wisdom—or a good husband.

Six

PUTTING ON NEW LIFE

Most Christians do not have difficulty understanding the concept of salvation. It is quite straightforward: The Holy Spirit convicts you of going your own way instead of God's way, you understand that Jesus gave His life as a perfect sacrifice for your sin, you repent or turn away from your sin and ask God for forgiveness, and then you receive your new life by faith. It's an incredible miracle, but because we talk about it so much and so many people have been born again, it almost seems like no big deal.

Oh, maybe I shouldn't have said that! Actually, being rescued from hell and given heaven is a *very big deal!* But you probably can relate to what I'm saying, because the deeper truth of what's supposed to happen to people after their salvation experience leaves many scratching their heads.

From a human perspective, to be asked to live life as Jesus did is like being asked to swim across the Pacific Ocean. It's impossible! Let's not be foolish—it's tough to love people sacrificially, for example. None of us has enough innate desire or energy to consistently do that. But in our pride, we foolishly think maybe, kinda, perhaps we can. Not going to happen. We will crash and burn. Trying to live the Christian life in our natural strength and ability is a miserable experience.

So how is this supposed to work? The answer is not in trying to morph up the old you. You need a *new* you.

It's another topic Paul wanted to clear the air on in the letter he wrote to his Galatian friends. Here's what he said:

> I have been crucified with Christ and I no longer live, but Christ lives in me. The life I live in the body, I live by faith in the Son of God, who loved me and gave himself for me. I do not set aside the grace of God, for if righteousness could be gained through the law, Christ died for nothing! (2:20-21)

As we've already learned, the problem with the Galatians was that some misguided teachers were telling them they must follow the Jewish laws to be sure they were saved and pleasing God. "No, that's wrong," Paul insisted. And this led to his confrontation with *the* apostle Peter on this issue. (For more background on this, reread Galatians 2:1-14.)

So we have to figure out what Paul meant when he said that it really wasn't him living his life. Incredibly bizarre, don't you think? Somehow Paul was dead and yet alive in Christ at the same time. For sure Paul meant that gritting your teeth and forcing yourself to live up to the standard of the law was impossible. To live the life God seeks for us, we all need something none of us has or can acquire on our own.

The interesting thing is that, too much of the time, pumping ourselves up and trying to push the boulder up the hill just feels right. You might have said a time or two, maybe after hearing a motivating sermon in church, "All right, this is it. I am going to change my ways! Yep, I'm going to do it! Every day until Jesus comes or I pass on, I'm going to pray three hours and read twenty chapters in the Bible. This finally is it—the secret! No turning back for the rest of my days. God, you can count on me!" (I wonder if this is where God smiles knowingly.)

When you promise that sort of thing—even though it's a good idea and in practice could benefit you immensely—you are just setting a standard or "law" for yourself that you'll eventually break. And even if right now you are getting your back up and saying, "No, no, Ted! I actually *am doing* this, and just because you don't have much self-discipline and can't…!" Whoa, big fella! Let me tell you that even if you never miss a day of praying and reading the Bible for seventy-seven years—before dying from arthritic knees and fatal eye fatigue—you would have at least *one* day, and more likely quite a few, when you had a lousy attitude and didn't want to pray and read the Bible. Your heart motivation stunk, so in the true reality, you failed and broke your own law. When you appear before God, you will not be able to say, "See, I told you I could do it."

Ultimately, every law accomplishes that goal, proving that we are all lawbreakers. A law will point out that you are a sinful person, because you can't pray and read the Bible that much or do anything indefinitely in your own strength without messing up. But if you die to your old sin nature and allow the life of God Himself to flow into you and occupy you, then you can live an incredible life, because Christ will be living His perfect, God-honoring life through you.

I'm not going to turn into a Greek scholar on you, but when Paul said, "I have been crucified with Christ," it is important to understand the verb tense he was using in the original language. "I have been crucified with Christ" is stated in the perfect tense. So it could be accurately translated, "I have been and *continue to be* crucified with Christ." This helps us know why the apostle Paul once revealed a puzzling personal detail about himself, "I die every day" (1 Corinthians 15:31).

It also explains why the Bible, when it talks about being filled with the Spirit, always uses that same perfect verb tense: We "have been filled and continue to be filled." So if you are filled with the Holy Spirit on Thursday and do mighty things in His power, don't expect that you will have the same anointing when you climb out of bed on Friday. Each new day requires a new filling—and that includes Sundays. In fact, you want to be especially sure you fill up on Sunday morning, because I've noticed that Satan and his demons seem to show up at church to mess with people for tactical reasons!

This Haggardism addresses both nutritional and spiritual issues: *Wheaties are hard to beat in the morning, but even better for you is to get up and fill up with the Holy Spirit.*

The Christian life you want to live is like an enormous diesel engine sucking up barrels of fuel twenty-four hours a day, every day. If you don't keep filling the tank, the engine's going to sputter. We are to constantly continue being filled with the Spirit and growing in God.

There is no such thing as a free ride in the Christian life. When we get to heaven, we won't have to struggle with sin anymore. There will be no need to refuel with the Holy Spirit. That will be great, because I am a world-class sinner. And even though I may not have met you, I'll go out on a limb and say, "So are you!"

Let's not kid ourselves. Yes, we have an ultimate answer to our sin: the blood of Jesus. But we are not rid of the foul sin stuff. We may even be tempted to think that our heroes in the faith—dead or alive—don't have issues with their sin side. Don't believe it. Remember how our man Paul said that he was the "worst" of sinners? This guy did not say things like that just to keep his tongue and lips warmed up. He was deadly serious. All great saints humbly recognize their powerlessness to defeat the old sin nature and live the Christlike life on their own. I'll give you an example.

Some years ago I had the opportunity to attend a meeting in which Dr. David Yonggi Cho of South Korea spoke. If anyone could climb out of the sin pit, you would think it might be Dr. Cho—he pastors one of the largest churches in the world. When I heard him speak, his church had 763,000 members! My, my, that's a lot of candles for the Christmas Eve services.

When Dr. Cho got up to speak and said that he prays three hours every morning, I thought, *That makes sense. Cho is so godly and such a successful pastor. He probably spends the whole time just having a nice buddy-buddy talk with the Lord.* Later I heard the rest of the story during the Q-and-A segment of this meeting with Dr. Cho. Someone asked him, "Dr. Cho, why do you pray three hours every day?"

He gave us two reasons. First, he said that it takes a lot of spiritual strength and authority to pastor 763,000 people. The church had ministry throughout the world, *80,000* cell groups, a huge staff—on and on it went. Dr. Cho explained with great candor the incredible temptations he faced. "The church doesn't pay me what I am worth," he said, "and I suffer horrible temptation from time to time to steal the tithe from God."

Then Dr. Cho dropped the "Bunker Buster." He said that the second reason he needed to pray three hours a day was because he was "so bad." Really? You can imagine how quiet it got in the room. Dr. Cho told how much he "hates people." It was almost funny—here's this famous, really nice Korean pastor saying, "I have to spend hours in prayer every morning, because I need to forgive these people I hate." He listed some of the people he hated, including the elders in his church. "Even in my dreams I don't want to be with those people!" he said.

I hope you are catching the drift of this. Here's one of the great men of God of our day admitting that he struggles mightily to keep sin controlled in his life.

Dr. Cho told us that he had needed every minute of those three hours of prayer because of his old sin nature, the devil's attacks, his powerlessness without the Spirit, and his need for the fruit and gifts of God. "I can't have any of them unless God gives them to me," he said.

We all wonder, I'm sure, "Why does life have to work this way?" Good question. It's all related to our old sin nature. Here's how Paul described it in another letter:

> You were taught, with regard to your former way of life, to put off your old self, which is being corrupted by its deceitful desires; to be made new in the attitude of your minds; and to put on the new self, created to be like God in true righteousness and holiness. (Ephesians 4:22-24)

There it is. We have to "put off the old"—kill the old sin nature, put off the devil's plan for our lives, and put on the new, Christ-controlled, empowered self.

ASSASSINATE SIN

The way sin in us has more lives than a cat reminds me of an old movie called *The Hand*. I saw it when I was a boy, and it was so scary, I still shiver when I think about it. In the movie, "the hand" just won't die. The actors threw the hand in the fireplace, but it crawled out and grabbed a guy's throat. Then they threw the hand outside, but it crawled through the snow and grabbed somebody again. It just kept coming back to life! The sin nature is like "the hand." You can hit it, beat it, pound it, fry it, drown it, freeze it—you can do everything to it! But it just keeps reviving. That's why we have to kill it every day.

You might ask, "Okay, how does this work? Cut to the chase, Ted. What does all of this look like in a real person's life?"

I know there are a number of ways to confront the old sin nature. Here's mine: It is my habit and practice 90 percent or more of the time to get up in the morning and, as I said earlier, "commit suicide." Like Paul, I make an effort to die daily to my flesh. I do this because I know that when the *King James Version* calls me to "mortify the deeds of the body" (Romans 8:13), it is as positive for spiritual health as a trip to the gym is for physical health. *Mortification* means to put down, to take off, to kill the old sin nature.

There are at least two reasons I suggest you get in your prayer closet every day and wage war on the old sin nature. First, because it's an honor as well as a noble thing to use our privilege to talk to God one on one. That's a great motivation, but there's another one we should all have: *We must pray because we are so bad.*

Here's my spiritual workout after I get up in the morning. I first stir up the gifts of God that are within me, the things He has promised me that give me strength. You and I don't need any additional endowment of power—we have the very power of God already; why would we need more? But we do need to stir it up or activate it. And the more we do this, the better we'll get at it.

Then, while I am doing that stirring up of power, I also kill the old sin nature.

I do this every day because I am a sinful person. Everyone has this core issue. I regret if you find that offensive, but it happens to be true. If you want to know how evil I am, read through any of the Bible's sin lists. If you let it, that old sin nature will dominate and destroy your life. Even if you've been born again, your sin nature can make you mean, bitter, and angry. Think about it. We all know some pretty mean "Christians." Your old sin nature can cause you to lie and become immoral. It will cause you to do things that will bring shame to you and to those you love. If the old sin nature takes charge, nothing positive will result.

So I suggest that first thing every morning, you get up and kill the old sin nature.

Next, in your prayer time, as you seek to allow Christ to be predominant in your life, announce to the devil and his demons that they have no authority or control over you. Tell the Enemy, "Nope, in the name of Jesus, there's no room for you today."

As you deal with these two big battlefronts—the old sin nature and any demonic activity around you—fill up to the brim with the Holy Spirit. This may take twenty minutes, an hour, or three hours. I need about an hour to closely connect and get into good-flowing communication with the Spirit—and I usually want more time than that. That's me—I'm a senior pastor with a big sin problem. The process and time required may differ for you.

When I am filling up with the Holy Spirit, I like to pray through the fruit of the Spirit listed in Galatians 5:22-23. Here's an example of how I pray:

> Father, in the name of Jesus, give me the love, joy, peace,
> patience, kindness, goodness, faithfulness, gentleness, and

self-control I need today to live life to the fullest, in the way
You want me to live. Fill me up to overflowing with Your
Spirit so that I will produce all of this fruit in every word
and action.

That's how you and I appropriate God's Spirit and see the fruit.
So, for example, if you need an abundance of self-control in your life
on a particular day, fill up with the Holy Spirit so that the resulting
fruit is self-control.

Next, as my day begins, I often pray through the gifts of the Spirit
listed in 1 Corinthians 12:8-10. I ask for wisdom and knowledge to
work in me in a powerful way. I cry out for faith and confidence in
God to flow in every area of my life. I ask for the healing I need, and
that I can pass it on to the sick and hurting I'll encounter that day.
Since I've been told to "eagerly desire spiritual gifts" (1 Corinthians
14:1), I earnestly seek to receive miraculous powers and to know how
to discern spirits. In fact, I want them all—tongues, interpretations,
and prophecy. Here's how I pray through some of the gifts of the Spirit:

Father, in the name of Jesus, when I am talking to people, I
want to say what You want me to say. As I go through the day,
I want to be discerning and know whether people are lying to
me or not. I want to know if I'm encountering a lot of angelic
activity and demonic activity. In the situations I face today,
give me wisdom and knowledge. Let the beautiful gift of faith
operate in me. I love Your fantastic gifts of healing, and I want
to flow in miracles today. Oh, God, I so earnestly desire to
receive and use all the spiritual gifts.

So that is how the Christian life really happens. It does not come by tightening our belts on our crumbling, weak, failing old lives. It's the new life of Christ operating in and through us. It's Jesus in you, because you are the temple of the Holy Spirit. So it's Jesus's holiness, righteousness, love, joy, peace, patience, kindness, goodness, faithfulness, gentleness, and self-control.

I don't know about you, but I find it appealing to walk around looking like Ted Haggard but having the amazing Holy Spirit empowering me to live the life God desires for me. That's how a kid who grew up on a pig farm in Indiana can actually do something that matters in this world. Oh, man, is this cool or what?

In other words, Jesus comes and says, "Step aside, friend. You can't do it, so I'll do it for you!" Is that a great deal or what? Don't you love this Guy? It's so incredible! That's why, when you get with the program, living the Spirit-filled life is not work. It's actually resting, like being in a sailboat propelled by the wind across a vast sea. The Spirit-filled life is not hard, it's easy! That's why, if you have a natural lazy streak like me, it's the only way to go! Be filled with the Holy Spirit; don't try to gain your righteousness through harsh obedience.

C. S. Lewis wrote in *Mere Christianity:*

> That is why the real problem of the Christian life comes
> where people do not usually look for it. It comes the very
> moment you wake up each morning. All of your wishes
> and hopes for the day rush at you like wild animals. And
> the first job each morning consists simply in shoving them
> all back; in listening to that other voice, taking that other
> point of view, letting that other larger, stronger, quieter life

come flowing in. And so on, all day. Standing back from all your natural fussings and frettings, coming in out of the wind.*

Well said, C. S.
What do you say we "put on some new life"?

---

* C. S. Lewis, *Mere Christianity* (New York: Macmillan, 1952), 167-68.

Questions for Pastor Ted

Daily life is a struggle. How do I keep focused on what the Lord wants me to do on a daily basis?

Suffering is part of life on earth, but it doesn't have to define us. Do what you can to get some of the Word and the Spirit alive in you first thing in the morning. After that, go about the work at hand. Be faithful in the small things. Do everything as unto the Lord. Do good work. God will be with you. He promises to never leave you or forsake you. He understands difficult times, and He will reward you either in this life or in the life to come.

I believe that speaking in tongues and using personal prayer languages are powerful gifts of the Holy Spirit that are available to all Christians, but I don't see this as an absolute worth splitting a church. But what if someone is really dogmatic about something like this and is in a strong position of influence? Do we have a responsibility to correct people in light of their potential to influence others?

Again, I think it depends on your relationship with the person. I am careful about commenting on things if I haven't been asked. If you are in a position of authority in people's lives, your responsibility to speak with them is heightened. Sometimes, though, they just need time. Very often, they will discover their error over a period of years and will moderate their thinking and teaching. Have you noticed how an old man will sit around and not say much? It's because he realizes that most of what people say is foolishness, and it's best to just stay quiet. Maybe we all need to learn from the old men.

Seven

COMPLETE THE GOSPEL

There's more to the gospel than meets the eye.

Do we limit its full impact by thinking the good news is only about salvation from sin? No doubt we're all grateful that the gospel does bring good news on the sin mess. But there's more.

People are in all kinds of trouble, and the gospel compels us to address every type of need. The leaders in the early church knew this. Paul knew it. Do we contemporary evangelical Christians know it?

Not long after Jesus began His ministry, He went one Sabbath to His home synagogue and read from the book of Isaiah—words recorded hundreds of years earlier by the prophet that were coming true about Jesus even as He held the scroll:

> The Spirit of the Lord is on me,
>> because he has anointed me
>> to preach good news to the poor.
> He has sent me to proclaim freedom for the prisoners
>> and recovery of sight for the blind,
> to release the oppressed,
>> to proclaim the year of the Lord's favor. (Luke 4:18-19)

Notice the breadth of what Jesus was anointed to do. The gospel touches and transforms all of life. It heals physical wounds, fights oppression, proclaims favor. It's good news for *everyone*. So what this means for us is that to complete the work of the gospel, we will find ourselves doing all kinds of things with all kinds of people. And that includes—maybe even begins with—assisting the poor.

When Paul went to Jerusalem to discuss his ministry with church leaders (see Galatians 2:1-10), the men in charge—James, Peter, and John—concluded that Paul's work with the Gentiles was going remarkably well. Apparently, the apostles offered him little specific feedback except the following, which Paul reported: "All they asked was that we should continue to remember the poor, the very thing I was eager to do" (verse 10).

God's mandate concerning the poor has not changed. We need to care for those who have less than we do. And the "less" is not just in reference to money or material stuff, though that is a big part of it. The poor among us are people who are in need financially *as well as* spiritually, physically, emotionally, mentally, and morally.

We are the people of God. We have His Spirit alive in us. We are here to continue His mission of realizing the kingdom of God. We have been given the DNA of our Father in heaven. That means we have the potential to be world-class givers and to effectively "remember the poor."

How are we to go about doing this? We have to be on the lookout for poverty wherever we find it, and then we have to work together to combine our resources to meet great needs.

I was reminded of this in a fresh way by a sad incident I witnessed one Sunday after services at New Life Church. It illustrates this idea that the scope of being poor is often larger than we think.

I'm a senior pastor and love my job, which means I like hanging out at the church building. As is often the case, one Sunday morning I was about the last person in the building, when I spotted two high-school kids, a boy and girl, standing inside the front doors, looking out at the driveway, waiting, I assumed, for their parents to pick them up.

The young man was at ease and carefree, but since girls seem more anxious in situations like this, I was prompted to say to the young woman, "Well, if your dad doesn't get here for some reason, tell one of the church hospitality people here to call me at home. I live just about a mile from the church, and I or my wife or one of my kids will bring some lunch up to you. Then, if you want, you can stay here in the church and rest on a couch. Maybe just hang out until the service tonight—you'll be okay."

"Thanks," she said, and we chatted a little bit.

I was distracted by someone else, and in the meantime a car pulled up. The man driving was her dad. He swung his door open and lurched out of the car as the girl walked toward him. He started yelling loudly at his daughter, even though she said, "Well, Daddy, I was looking for you and couldn't find you."

His face turned red, and he yelled at her, "You blankety-blank..."—what he said was disgusting. And when he got near her, he started hitting her with his fists, right under the canopy at the church entrance. I turned and walked toward him, shouting, "Stop that! You can't do that here!"

It turned into quite a confrontation, and a few other stragglers still on the church property heard my voice and gathered around. I yelled for someone to call the police as I approached the man and ordered him off the property. He stormed back to his car, still screaming at his daughter and me. I noticed a couple of other women in the car holding Bibles and looking scared, mighty scared. The high-school girl got into the car, and she was sobbing, her upper body heaving. You can only guess—if her father would hit her like that in front of me, what was happening behind closed doors at home?

As the man drove away, a few other men in the church and I heard him screaming at her. Even when he turned out of the parking lot, we still heard his angry words. He was enraged, totally out of control. I feared that if he had a gun, he would shoot her—and then probably come looking for me.

I drove home angry and upset because of what had happened. I thought about how foolish the man was. I thought about the fear, anxiety, and confusion that his family had to be feeling. I thought about the incident all afternoon. Apparently, the women in his life were trying to attend church. The others had gone elsewhere that morning, and this daughter had wanted to come to our youth program or something. Maybe he had swung by earlier and couldn't find her because of the crowd. This had enraged him. He'd left and come back to get her and wanted to punish her for wasting ten or fifteen minutes of his time.

So I wondered, *God, what is it going to take for our church to reach a guy like that? How are we going to coax him into fellowship with people who can help him? Are we going to get him with a Jesus commercial during some raunchy TV show? What about a door-to-door Jesus video distribution? Will it take somebody prayer walking through his apartment complex or neighborhood? Could we attract him to a special Easter outreach like our church's Thorn production? Lord Jesus, how are we going to rescue that man and his family?*

The situation reconfirmed to me why I believe the local church should be a storehouse of kingdom resources. This is the role for the local church. Every tactic I had in mind was something none of us could do exclusively on our own; we'd have to work together. I also knew there were other tactics more suited to this man—ideas I might not think of but that might be natural for someone else in the church.

The poor are everywhere, and we need to be everywhere for them with the gospel. We need to combine our resources—our ideas, our time, our talents, our money—so a man like that angry dad cannot escape from the truth. If we gather our resources together in our local churches, we can get food to a child in Africa and healing to a father who's abusing his family in Colorado Springs.

Remembering the Poor

The apostle Paul knew Scripture, so he would have been well aware of how deeply God cares about the poor. Here's one example from the Bible:

> For six years you are to sow your fields and harvest the crops,
> but during the seventh year let the land lie unplowed and
> unused. Then the poor among your people may get food from
> it, and the wild animals may eat what they leave. Do the same
> with your vineyard and your olive grove. (Exodus 23:10-11)

Part of the message God wants us to get here is that we really don't own all our stuff. God has rights to it, and He can tell us what to do with it so that others in need can be taken care of. Another verse along these lines is in Deuteronomy:

If there is a poor man among your brothers in any of the
towns of the land the LORD your God is giving you, do not be
hardhearted or tightfisted toward your poor brother. Rather be
openhanded and freely lend him whatever he needs. (15:7-8)

In other words, give generously to others. Clear enough! Here's
another Bible position on the poor:

"He defended the cause of the poor and needy,
    and so all went well.
Is that not what it means to know me?"
    declares the LORD. (Jeremiah 22:16)

God expects us to identify with and defend those who are less fortunate. He expects us to find them, help them, and deliver them. So
you see, this is one of those simple, black-and-white, no-questions-
asked issues. There are people in need all over the world, and God
wants us to do what we can to meet their needs.

Okay, okay. This is all well and good. It's easier said than done,
though, and, in fact, some go to great lengths to avoid the issue
entirely. For starters, we love our stuff, and we want more of it. Which
is why Jesus's encounter with a young man relates to us today, especially for many of us who are rich compared to most people in the rest
of the world. The details:

As Jesus started on his way, a man ran up to him and fell on
his knees before him. "Good teacher," he asked, "what must I
do to inherit eternal life?"

    "Why do you call me good?" Jesus answered. "No one is

good—except God alone. You know the commandments:
'Do not murder, do not commit adultery, do not steal, do not
give false testimony, do not defraud, honor your father and
mother.'"

"Teacher," he declared, "all these I have kept since I was
a boy."

Jesus looked at him and loved him. "One thing you lack,"
he said. "Go, sell everything you have and give to the poor,
and you will have treasure in heaven. Then come, follow me."
(Mark 10:17-21)

As we know, this man was unable to part with his wealth. And
after the man trudged away sadly, Jesus remarked to His disciples,
"Children, how hard it is to enter the kingdom of God! It is easier for
a camel to go through the eye of a needle than for a rich man to enter
the kingdom of God" (verse 24).

What? Was Jesus saying indirectly that people of means are in big
trouble with God? That could be bad news for you and me, because
those of us who live in the Western world, America in particular—
even if we feel we have only a modest income—are among the wealth-
iest people alive today. Thankfully, there's more to this story. Let me
explain what a camel going through the eye of a needle means.

In the Middle East, walls are built to enclose everything from
entire cities to family homes. Walls not only provide security from
thieves but are also used to keep large animals—such as horses, cattle,
and camels—from roaming into your living room. Since at times
these animals still need to be herded in and out, small archways called
"the eye of the needle" are cut in the walls. When people want to go
through one of these passageways, they have to stoop and shuffle

through. I have walked through these in Israel. It's a bit uncomfortable, but you can do it.

Getting a camel through the eye of a needle, though, is more of a task. Two things are required: First, the camel has to be so thirsty that its hump looks more like a lump. Second, the camel has to kneel. The camel jockey then prods the animal along, forcing it to shuffle and wiggle on its knees through the eye of a needle.

So part of the meaning of what Jesus said is, "Sure, a rich person can be saved. But it is a challenging effort, because it's especially tough for that person to be *thirsty* and *humble*."

The disciples would have understood what Jesus meant, but they were still shaken by His teaching. Even today we have a hard time with Jesus's words. After all, if rich people have a hard time getting something valuable, what chance does anyone else have?

"Who then can be saved?" the disciples asked Jesus. He had a very good answer for them that should comfort us as well: "With man this is impossible, but not with God; all things are possible with God" (verses 26-27).

And here is the rub: We can't save ourselves, whether we have diverse investments and vacation homes in Aspen or can barely afford to pay our rent. We are doomed either way, but God loves us a lot and wants us to spend eternity with Him.

I love the little phrase that revealed Jesus's attitude when He was dealing with the young ruler. It says simply that Jesus looked at him and "loved him." We need to remember that Jesus was not out to get this guy, to somehow make the man's life worse by laying a heavy burden on him. Jesus loved this rich young man and was trying to show him the way to real life. The Haggardized version of this would read, "Listen. Get rid of all your stuff. You are trusting in it too much.

Don't depend on it. End the stress and hassle. Give it all to the poor. That's a very good thing that our Father in heaven enjoys and rewards. You will be satisfied, and God will bless you for it."

Jesus was not advocating universal poverty and condemning prosperity. He was making clear that we all need to be careful where we put our trust. Another time He said, "You cannot serve both God and Money" (Matthew 6:24). We have to choose. And though it's tough to really live it out, I think we can agree that the choice is clear. God loves us, and in the end we'll be a lot richer for having trusted Him. So let's do what He wants—steadily, consistently promote the kingdom of God, take care of the needy, and love and care for other people in the same way we take care of ourselves.

How to Give

There is a right way and wrong way to express our generosity. Jesus explained:

> So when you give to the needy, do not announce it with trumpets, as the hypocrites do in the synagogues and on the streets, to be honored by men. (Matthew 6:2)

We are not to give so that people will notice it and say, "Thank you for being so generous." If we do that, it doesn't really count with God. Jesus explained very clearly that if we give so that others will honor us, then that is the extent of our reward:

> I tell you the truth, they have received their reward in full. But when you give to the needy, do not let your left hand

know what your right hand is doing, so that your giving may be in secret. Then your Father, who sees what is done in secret, will reward you. (verses 2-4) (*Note:* Many translations add one more important word at the end—"will reward you *openly.*")

I'll be blunt: Let's say that a pastor or someone from a parachurch ministry comes to you asking for a financial gift to do something for the kingdom of God, and you say, "Okay, I'll give you X dollars." Now if that person replies, "Oh, that's fantastic. For that amount we're going to put up a plaque in your name," double-knot your shoelaces and take off running. It all sounds so good, but be wary. Tell the person to forget the plaque. Don't blow your horn or let others blow it for you. Instead, give quietly, peacefully, unobtrusively—with a joyful heart. Don't allow the church or ministry to add your name to the major donors list. Don't attend major donor's functions. Don't let people convince you that you are special or have a unique calling because you are wealthy.

If, in fact, you *are* wealthy, keep a low profile. Give your entire tithe, no matter how large it is, to your local church. Let your church worry about how to spend it. Trust the judgment of the leaders, since this is the church you and your family have chosen to attend. This is where you have put down roots, where you intend to settle in with people who will become lifelong friends. Your tithe is God's, not yours. And 100 percent of the tithe should go to the general fund of your local church instead of special church projects. If your wealth and the size of your tithe come to the attention of church leaders, you might be asked to serve on the church board. But instead of taking a governing position, you might choose to find some other position of service. Your heart may best be guarded from pride by quietly teaching in the third-grade Sunday-school class or filling some other inconspicuous position.

If you have additional money you want to give above your tithe amount, give it as a general offering to your church, make a designated gift to some church project, or select a trustworthy parachurch ministry. But don't let any group exalt you or give you special treatment. If you like the special treatment or believe that you are a "high-capacity donor" with unique insight, you might, instead, be a candidate for the lesser reward of worldly, rather than heavenly, recognition.

I will not discuss choosing churches and selecting trustworthy parachurch ministries in this book, but I can give you a couple of quick guidelines. When choosing your local church, make sure that church knows the importance of being born again, believes that the Bible is the Word of God and that Jesus is the Son of God, and gives to the poor. From this foundation, you can select a church that's right for you. In my book *The Life-Giving Church,* I describe in detail the characteristics of a good church.

When checking out parachurch organizations, choose a ministry that advances the causes you believe in; then send an offering rather than a tithe. Your tithe belongs to the storehouse of your local church.

In your giving, though, don't let anybody tamper with your heart and steal the glory that God wants to give you for taking care of the poor and needy. Skip the brass bands. Give in secret, and your reward will come from your heavenly Father.

Those of us who are church or parachurch leaders have too often resorted to sinful foolishness in order to raise money for good, godly causes. If the only way we can raise enough money to get our church building built and collect offerings to care for the poor people is to coddle up to wealthy people, we need someone to take us behind the barn for a paddling. If questionable fund-raising techniques are required to raise money, it's a reflection on both the Christian leadership that is willing to use these methods and those who willingly succumb to them. Shame on us if we are that faithless.

Scripture promises that if we show favoritism to wealthy people by treating them in a special way, we're sinning (see James 2:1-11). No future in that!

We need to obey what the Bible teaches and encourage all people—poor, rich, and in between—to tithe and receive God's blessings as a result.

As a pastor of a growing church in which there's always a need for more cash, I've had people say, "Ted, when people give a significant amount, they need to get a personal phone call from you." But honestly, if I were going to make any such calls, I would rather call people who earned ten dollars and gave one dollar than those who earned one hundred thousand dollars and gave one thousand. In such an instance, it seems to me that giving the one dollar might actually require a larger sacrifice. But either way, I choose not to make such phone calls. Actually, as a senior pastor, I don't check people's giving records. I believe people give to God, and it's between God and them. An exception to this is when a church member needs financial assistance, and I check to see if the person has given to the church in the past. Or if someone is a candidate for leadership in the church, I might check to see if this person tithes. In both of these cases, people don't know I've checked, and I don't tell them, but sometimes what I discover when checking influences my decision.

The Mighty Mite

One of my favorite Bible stories is the one about the poor widow who was an incredibly sacrificial giver but would never get her name on a plaque. I love what she did because it helps you and me evaluate what to give and how we should give.

> As he taught, Jesus said, "Watch out for the teachers of the law. They like to walk around in flowing robes and be greeted in the marketplaces [in other words, they like to show off], and have the most important seats in the synagogues and the places of honor at banquets. They devour widows' houses and for a show make lengthy prayers." (Mark 12:38-40)

In case you missed it, Jesus had zero respect for these guys. Even their prayers were futile; these guys were not connecting positively with God. Jesus exposed their motives and said, "Don't do what they are doing—these people are exploiting widows. They are not taking care of people." Then He said ominously, "Such men will be punished most severely" (verse 40).

There's more to the story. Next, Jesus sat down opposite the offering boxes in the temple. Many churches have boxes like that, in which tithes and gifts can be deposited. Jesus watched as people came by and dropped in their money. Many rich people gave large amounts. There was nothing wrong with that; Jesus did not criticize these well-to-do people for their gifts. But then something remarkable happened:

> A poor widow came and put in two very small copper coins, worth only a fraction of a penny.

Calling his disciples to him, Jesus said, "I tell you the
truth, this poor widow has put more into the treasury than
all the others. They all gave out of their wealth; but she, out
of her poverty, put in everything—all she had to live on."
(verses 42-44)

This woman's actions both inspire and convict. As the years have
gone by, Gayle and I have been increasingly blessed and able to give
more and more into the kingdom of God. We enjoy giving our tithe
and special offerings most of the time. Other times we are pressed
financially but have decided that this is a principle in God's Word that
we'll consistently live by. For years now we've taught people to tithe
faithfully to their local church.

I know, I know. I can hear some of you questioning the tithe for
New Testament believers. Followers of the God of Abraham, Isaac,
and Jacob have always tithed. Jewish believers tithe, the early church
tithed, and there is nothing in the Bible that indicates that worshipers
of God don't tithe. It's inherent in who we are.

I believe that God gives a vision and purpose to every church and
that He adds people to the church. Since the church is responsible to
fulfill 100 percent of the vision and purpose God has given it, when
those who attend that church tithe, the leadership of the church will
have 100 percent of the resources needed to fulfill the church's calling.
But if 60 percent of the people tithe, the church will only have 60 percent of the required resources. The result is what I refer to as a 40 percent frustration level. A church's frustration level equals the percent of
people who give only when they want to and, consequently, often
withhold from the storehouse, thus denying the church's leadership
the consistent resources needed for that church to function according

to God's plan. So if only 10 percent of the people tithe, the leadership will deal with a 90 percent frustration level. Conversely, if 100 percent of the people tithe, there will be an abundance in that storehouse, and God's perfect vision and purpose will be fully funded.

Another thing that motivates me to tithe is the fact that Judas was the treasurer for Jesus. Because we know the end of the story, we have a jaundiced view of Judas. But remember that he was highly respected by the other disciples. When Jesus said that one of His disciples was going to betray Him, no one looked at Judas. Actually, each of them contemplated whether it might be himself. It's interesting that the other disciples respected Judas so highly until we think about his only known offense prior to betraying Christ: He took liberties with Jesus's money. He diverted God's money to projects that he thought were good (see John 12:6). Judas did exactly what we do when we don't tithe. Hmm.

Finally, I know that God is sovereign and powerful and wants certain things done on the earth. I also know that God is going to use His people to fund His storehouses through the tithe and other projects through offerings. Since He is going to do this, I want to communicate to Him that when He sends funds my way, I will tithe faithfully. I don't have to be convinced, motivated, cajoled, or visited in order to give. I don't have to hear a voice or see pictures and understand a new vision in order to give.

A pithy Haggardism: *I am a Christian. Therefore, I give.*

For us to faithfully give, it does take believing. The widow's giving approach is very challenging. When most of us reflect on her "mighty mite," we think, *Man, I can't do that! I don't even want to think about it.* But we need to remind ourselves that "with God all things are possible" (Matthew 19:26). We can give because He wants to give through us.

So let me suggest some guidelines I try to follow as I give and seek to remember the poor, thereby helping "complete the gospel":

- If I go to a meeting, and those in charge give an over-the-top spiel and try to pull all my emotional strings, I never give. The hype is not necessary. Let the Holy Spirit woo and convince. Then we givers are happy campers, because we weren't manipulated into giving.

- If people raising money try to convince me that they are tapping into some spiritual insight like the gift of prophecy to raise money, I never give. Give me a break. That kind of thing can be so gross. They may say something like, "God is showing me that there are twelve people here tonight who are each going to give a thousand dollars." I am not impressed; in fact, it borders on spiritual manipulation. They may be nice, well-meaning people, but I'm not going to give the Lord's money to support such nonsense.

- If someone has dipped into tithe and offering money given to the storehouse of a local church to pay for a fund-raising campaign, I never give. How can we know? Ask!

On a more positive note, here's what I do: I tithe to my local church because it supports the poor all over the world. If my local church didn't support the poor everywhere, I would switch churches. And if I didn't have that option, this would be the time to become a board member or key leader in the church I attend in order to try to change its values from the top down.

And, as I've already mentioned, in addition to tithing we should give gifts and offerings to special projects. At New Life Church I love to challenge the congregation on an occasional Sunday morning— "Hey, everybody, we've heard there are kids in Afghanistan who need blankets. It's getting cold there, and they are freezing at night. Let's take an offering." So we pass the baskets a second time—after we've collected our tithes—and people dig deeper. Out of love for the poor, we give some more. It's amazing what the body of Christ can accomplish when we work together like that.

I believe if we follow these simple guidelines and do not reward those who use gimmicks to raise money, the church will have what it needs to care for the poor and advance the kingdom of God. Don't feed the fund-raising monsters. Just steadily supply the storehouse at your local church.

God smiles on us when we give the way He does and remember the poor.

Questions for Pastor Ted

I love the Lord with all my heart. I want to serve Him and the body, but I don't feel I am qualified enough to serve my church the way I want to. What is wrong with me?

Nothing is wrong with you except the fact that you are wrong! Everyone has strengths and weaknesses. You are letting your weaknesses define you. Many people are limited in what they can do just because they are afraid of what they *cannot* do. Here is the truth: Everyone starts out unqualified. The way you become qualified is to start and then learn as you go. Don't be stubborn. Instead, follow the lessons of a child. If babies didn't want to try to walk because they couldn't run like a football player, they would never begin. The process goes like this: Walk, fall, walk, fall, walk, fall, walk, run. Babies naturally do the little they can in the beginning, and eventually they walk and run. Do the same. Do the little you can, and let God develop you. Do the little you can as a confident servant of Christ, and His church will be grateful.

I want to give to the poor, but I am a single parent and can hardly make ends meet. What can I do?

The single greatest thing we can do to help people from all walks of life is to help build healthy life-giving churches. So even though you are struggling financially, be sure to tithe and participate in your local church. That church can then use its corporate strength to help the poor.

Second, if you want to do something more specific, do kind

things for the poor. As soon as your kids are old enough, volunteer as a family to help out at the local soup kitchen—maybe at Thanksgiving or Christmas—and serve those in need. I would encourage you to be careful, though, as a single mom, about developing personal relationships with needy individuals, because of your responsibility to protect your children. However, if you meet a needy family in your church whom you can assist, that might be a safer option. Do not, however, bring strangers into your home until your children are grown. Serve the poor with others at church or at the soup kitchen, but not in your home.

I know someone may accuse me of violating the biblical exhortation about showing hospitality, so let me clarify what I'm saying. You are your children's only parent, which means that the level of protection and security God desires for them at home is already cut in half. It is so important that children feel extremely safe in their homes. If you, as a single parent, allow strangers into your home, you are compromising your role as a good parent.

I know of too many situations in which children were abused, abducted, and even murdered because compassionate parents allowed the security of their home to be compromised. If you're a single or married adult without children, then it's your call. But as a single mom with kids, *no way!* Once your kids are grown and you are at home with no one else to protect, you can decide whether you want to show hospitality to strangers. But for now you need to be involved in helping the poor through the efforts of your church or some other organization dedicated to helping those in need.

Eight

FOOLISH OR WISE—IT'S OUR CHOICE

"Every child is born a fool," my grandmother used to say.

Was she just a crotchety old grump? No, she was actually a nice lady who liked kids—even wild little Teddy. What she meant by her tangy motto was that nobody gets wisdom without earning it. It's a process we can't avoid, one that involves many choices. And the choices we make will determine whether we are foolish or wise.

In the spiritual dimension—which impacts everything we think, feel, say, and do—there are clearly marked paths that will result in wise or foolish living. It's up to us. If we want to be foolish no more, we need to take to heart words like these:

> You foolish Galatians! Who has bewitched you? Before your
> very eyes Jesus Christ was clearly portrayed as crucified. I would
> like to learn just one thing from you: Did you receive the Spirit
> by observing the law, or by believing what you heard? Are you
> so foolish? After beginning with the Spirit, are you now trying
> to attain your goal by human effort? (Galatians 3:1-3)

The Bible has a lot to say about these two ways of life. Decision after decision, large or small, we decide, "Will I be foolish or wise?"

Being foolish is more than just saying dumb things to one another when we are angry or frustrated. There really is a state of foolishness—no, it's not California—and it's inside our heads and hearts! Some people, based on an ongoing pattern of how they think and act, are bona-fide, card-carrying, certified *fools*. On the opposite pole, there are people who make good decisions and do the right thing most of the time. They deserve to be called *wise*.

How do we know whether we are wise or foolish? Well, we determine on a daily basis what path we will follow. We must constantly ask ourselves, "Okay, am I gaining wisdom? Is my life getting better? Do I know how to gain wisdom, or am I just living life hoping that good things will happen to me? Do I really want to grow in wisdom and enjoy the life God has planned for me? Is my life random or intentional? God created an orderly universe with wisdom; is my life becoming orderly with wisdom as well?"

In the Bible the book of Proverbs is a gold mine of information on the topics of foolishness and wisdom. If you will study and apply to your life even the first nine chapters of Proverbs, you will earn the equivalent of a bachelor's degree in wisdom.

In Proverbs, wisdom and folly are personified as two women who call out to a group of people called "the simple." If you are wondering who "the simple" are, well, let's pause for a moment and pull out our picture IDs! This is one club that bars no one based on any social, economic, racial, gender, or religious distinctions. "Y'all come down," is this group's mantra. We're all insiders, so don't be embarrassed by the label. But we "simples" must decide whether to respond to the call of wisdom or the call of folly. We can't just wander through life and hope it turns out okay. We can't be passive. That's about the best way possible to end up at Camp Folly. Proverbs 9 introduces Lady Wisdom first:

Wisdom has built her house;

> she has hewn out its seven pillars.

She has prepared her meat and mixed her wine;

> she has also set her table.

She has sent out her maids, and she calls

> from the highest point of the city.

"Let all who are simple come in here!"

> she says to those who lack judgment....

"Leave your simple ways and you will live;

> walk in the way of understanding." (verses 1-4,6)

The other female recruiter in Proverbs shows up a few verses later:

The woman Folly is loud;

> she is undisciplined and without knowledge.

She sits at the door of her house,

> on a seat at the highest point of the city,

calling out to those who pass by,

> who go straight on their way.

"Let all who are simple come in here!"

> she says to those who lack judgment.

"Stolen water is sweet;

> food eaten in secret is delicious!" [She's talking about
>
> > immoral and other sinful behavior.]

But little do they know that the dead are there,

> that her guests are in the depths of the grave. (verses 13-18)

Please get the picture that Proverbs is painting for us. The simple wander by and hear two voices. Both offer seemingly desirable things.

Both are certainly attractive. But Wisdom draws people to life and God's destiny for them, while Folly welcomes others to pressure, worry, anxiety, disappointment, and ultimately death.

So that we know precisely what to look for, let's take a closer look at the two options for "the simple."

THE FOOLISH AND THE WISE

Following are some insights from Scripture on foolishness and wisdom. You'll observe that the majority of the verses dealing with wisdom relate to how a person receives instruction, responds to discipline or to a harsh word, or uses his or her tongue. A wise person is someone who is *humble,* not *arrogant.* As for the foolish, well, you'll get a pretty good sense of them in these verses.

> The fool says in his heart,
>   "There is no God."
> They are corrupt, and their ways are vile;
>   there is no one who does good. (Psalm 53:1)

As if to give the point special emphasis, twice the Bible says, "The fool says in his heart, 'There is no God'" (see also Psalm 14:1). So when you hear somebody at work or in the media or anywhere say something like, "There is no God!"—well, you can count on the fact that this person does not embrace wisdom. It's interesting to me that those who claim to be wise, who believe that reason, science, or their own intellects have concluded that there is no God, are so obviously foolish. Often they will claim to be freethinkers when in reality they have wandered into the oldest trick—believing that they have the ability to comprehend an infinite God with their finite minds and proclaim that He doesn't exist. There is empirical evidence all around us that points to God as Creator. Only a person determined to deny facts and embrace fantasy can deny the existence of God. As a result, those who think of themselves as thoughtful and wise are instead, often notably, great fools.

A fool spurns his father's discipline,
>   but whoever heeds correction shows prudence. (Proverbs
>   15:5)

A mocker resents correction;
>   he will not consult the wise. (verse 12)

Accepting discipline is not just for kids, either. That's why you and I need to seek spiritual accountability with godly mentors and acquire a taste for correction in life. Wise people know how to respond to authority in society, in the family, in the church, and in the workplace. Fools, however, often find themselves in consternation over governmental authorities, become destructive forces within their families, are unable to cooperate in a community of faith, or are a burden to their supervisors at work. As I mentioned earlier, God has established His creation in order. As a result, the wise see God's hand in creation and appreciate evidence, research, science, and order. Fools deny that order and believe the universe is chaotic. God has established order for relationships. Fools challenge God's order in society, the family, the church, and the workplace, while the wise understand it, work with it, and utilize it to provide strength and safety for people.

A fool finds pleasure in evil conduct,

> but a man of understanding delights in wisdom.
>
>> (Proverbs 10:23)

Stay away from people who like to push the evil edge in what they watch on television, what they do with their free time, or what they talk and joke about. Fools don't comprehend how destructive personal behavior destroys their futures, their families, and the communities around them. Those who have gained wisdom, on the other hand, appreciate the constraints required by responsibility, so they can joyfully approach their futures as they live honorable lives that provide stability and consistency and communicate trustworthy life messages to others. Wisdom instructs people in joyful honor, while foolish living is selfish and unstable.

The wise in heart accept commands,

> but a chattering fool comes to ruin. (Proverbs 10:8)

The way of a fool seems right to him,

> but a wise man listens to advice. (Proverbs 12:15)

A wise person is connected to other people who are respected and know something—and he or she acts on what they say. Fools say, "Just do it!"—whatever seems right at the time. They listen only to themselves, sometimes because they're jabbering so much no one else can get a word in edgewise.

A wise man fears the LORD and shuns evil,

> but a fool is hotheaded and reckless. (Proverbs 14:16)

I've always told my kids that nothing good happens after midnight. By that I mean, "Stay home and away from evil." It's reckless to be places where, time after time, bad things tend to happen. Pay attention to this principle. It could save your life.

> The wise inherit honor,
>> but fools he [the Lord] holds up to shame.
>>> (Proverbs 3:35)

God wants to give us honor; He wants to bless us. But He will reveal fools for what they are.

> Do not rebuke a mocker or he will hate you;
>> rebuke a wise man and he will love you.
> Instruct a wise man and he will be wiser still;
>> teach a righteous man and he will add to his learning.
>>> (Proverbs 9:8-9)

Again, wise people are open to criticism and instruction. Foolish people have a more difficult time imagining that they are wrong.

> A wise son brings joy to his father,
>> but a foolish son grief to his mother. (Proverbs 10:1)

Do you have kids? Have you ever been someone's kid? 'Nuff said.

I am amazed as I grow older and see the incredible delight that comes to parents when their children love them and honor them. I'll never forget the first time our two oldest children, Christy and Marcus, were back from college and wanted to stay home with us instead of going out with their friends. I would never have expected it, but it did so much for both Gayle and me. I am becoming convinced that one of the greatest blessings in life for parents is to be able to be proud of their children. This applies to children of all ages. Our charge: Live lives of wisdom so that we will be a blessing to our parents and our family name.

> The wise woman builds her house,
>> but with her own hands the foolish one tears hers down.
>> (Proverbs 14:1)

Wise women contribute positively to those around them, including their husbands and children, and thus build up their houses. They are usually thoughtful and intentional in the process. I've observed that a foolish woman who is tearing down her house—that is, wrecking her marriage and family with some type of destructive behavior—often doesn't know or admit to what she's doing. She just can't see it because she thinks she's in the right. Fools often displace responsibility and seldom find fault within themselves.

> The lips of the wise spread knowledge;
>> not so the hearts of fools. (Proverbs 15:7)

Fools have not attained wisdom, so how can they pass along anything helpful or of value to others?

> Let the wise listen and add to their learning,
>> and let the discerning get guidance. (Proverbs 1:5)

The wise are not too proud to keep learning. The greatest leaders in the world are simply great students who now articulate what they have learned.

That's just a sampling of verses related to wisdom and foolishness, but I'm going to stop because I think you get the point. Scripture goes on and on and on about this subject. Why? Because it's essential.

I urge you to explore all the Bible has to say on these topics. You will be amazed at the benefits.

GROWING IN WISDOM

With that mini-education in wisdom versus foolishness completed, what's next? How do we grow in wisdom?

I trust I've convinced you that choosing wisdom is the way to go? (If not, please stop, do not pass Go. You need to reread all those verses!) So now I do have a—pardon the expression—"simple" four-idea plan for you to consider.

1. Hear and Do the Word

Becoming a truly wise person starts first with both *hearing and doing the Word of God.* I know that sounds obvious, but it is important, because some people read the Word of God but don't apply it. Others read the Word of God and forget it, because they are on a Bible-reading plan in which they rush through six chapters a day. When you are sailing along at that speed, it's harder to latch on to the big ideas of the Bible, to let the Holy Spirit help you understand and apply them.

Here's another Haggardism for you. Call it the Haggard Bible-reading plan: *Read the Bible; then do what it says!*

The story Jesus told of the wise and foolish builders explains a lot:

> Therefore everyone who hears these words of mine and puts
> them into practice is like a wise man who built his house on
> the rock. The rain came down, the streams rose, and the winds
> blew and beat against that house; yet it did not fall, because it
> had its foundation on the rock. But everyone who hears these
> words of mine and does not put them into practice is like a
> foolish man who built his house on sand. The rain came
> down, the streams rose, and the winds blew and beat against
> that house, and it fell with a great crash. (Matthew 7:24-27)

In this parable the "house" stands for our lives. At numerous times in our lives, the wind will blow, the streams will rise, the floods will threaten to wash away our houses. How well we survive those storms is decided by whether or not we listen to what the Bible says and apply it to our lives.

This need to "do" the Word (see James 1:22) is one reason I'm such a fan of small groups. In a healthy small group, we study the Scriptures together and then help and encourage one another to apply the truth at heart level.

Remember, every promise in the Word of God is conditional. If we'll fulfill the conditions, then the promises become a covenant that God will fulfill in our lives. Many people wonder why they are not receiving the clear promises in the Bible. Some speculate that God is withholding blessings from them. But God does not withhold from anyone. Instead, He always keeps His Word. All we have to do is align ourselves with His Word by fulfilling its conditions, or doing what it says.

2. Stay Full of the Spirit

A second way we can grow in wisdom is to *always be full of the Holy Spirit.* This is illustrated in Jesus's parable of the ten virgins. That certainly is a valid application. But here I want to emphasize the meaning of "being full," which mean always "tanking up" on wisdom and discernment in order to avoid foolishness.

I've discussed this before in the book, but I'll say it again: If we want to live powerful lives, it's critical that we get up in the morning, kill the old sin nature, and then fill up to the brim with the Holy Spirit. I urge you to open your heart to the river of God. Enjoy the guidance, counsel, and comfort of the Spirit. Serve Christ by employing the gifts of the Spirit. Let this energizing, refreshing life flow out in your life every day, all day.

Some may say, "Well, I took care of that when I was filled with the Spirit in 1977 at a camp meeting down in Kansas."

My response is, "Hmm. Then what?"

When it comes to connecting with God, I find it wise to keep things fresh. Having a great initial experience is wonderful, and if a person was filled up in 1977 and has kept being filled since then—and along the way has experienced some deliverance, healing, and victories over sin—that's one thing. But if someone thinks that God did all He could back in 1977 and then stepped out for a long coffee break, that's another matter.

The relationship God longs to have with us is intense, interactive, and dynamic. Here's the story Jesus told:

At that time the kingdom of heaven will be like ten virgins who took their lamps and went out to meet the bridegroom. Five of them were foolish and five were wise. The foolish ones took their lamps but did not take any oil with them. The wise, however, took oil in jars along with their lamps. The bridegroom was a long time in coming, and they all became drowsy and fell asleep.

At midnight the cry rang out: "Here's the bridegroom! Come out to meet him!"

Then all the virgins woke up and trimmed their lamps. The foolish ones said to the wise, "Give us some of your oil; our lamps are going out." (Matthew 25:1-8)

Now until this moment, all these virgins hanging out and waiting for the bridegroom looked pretty cool. Each one had her little lamp and was probably wearing the latest fashion. Life was good. But then at the most unexpected moment, guess what? The bridegroom showed up! How impolitic of him! This element of being caught off guard by events was true, too, in the story about the man who built his house on the sand. No thunderstorms had been predicted that day by Naomi the weather girl, but suddenly a black cloud formed and the rain gushed down. What a mess trying to rebuild a house's foundation in such lousy weather!

I think I'm on a roll. Here's another Haggardism: *We don't know what our Christianity is made of until the pressure's on.*

Pressure in life normally does not come when you are having your morning devotions. You can be in your pajamas, reading your Bible, still drowsy, coffee cup in hand—there's little danger or stress. But when you are on your way to work and somebody rear-ends your car—then you'll find out what you are like on the inside. If you are full of the Holy Spirit, you'll stay calm. If not, you better have your road-rage medication in the console.

The five virgins who weren't ready started scrambling:

The foolish ones said to the wise, "Give us some of your oil; our lamps are going out."

"No," they replied, "there may not be enough for both us and you. Instead, go to those who sell oil and buy some for yourselves."

But while they were on their way to buy the oil, the bridegroom arrived. The virgins who were ready went in with him to the wedding banquet. And the door was shut. (verses 8-10)

Do you see the parallel between this story and the one about the foolish builder? In both cases the pressure came, and some people were ready while others were not. One group succeeded. The other failed. These were equal-opportunity disasters.

I observe this same type of thing as I counsel people. Many people are in the midst of life storms, and I can tell that they have depended on others on the sunny days for their prayer life and inspiration. The sources may have been radio and TV preachers or Bible-series tapes. Others have fed themselves worship CDs and Christian books. (Ah, well, actually there's nothing wrong with a good Christian book as a supplement in life, don't you think?)

Here's what I've learned: Nothing will serve you as well as reading your own Bible and being filled with the Holy Spirit, hearing the voice of God in your heart and following His leading. Don't miss out! This is a big deal, because it's the difference between being wise and being foolish.

3. Align with God's Character

The third way to develop wisdom is to *maintain alignment with God's character*. We do this by spending time with Him in prayer and reading His Word. In His presence we are changed. His character or nature influences ours and imparts wisdom to us. It is God's method to clean people on the inside. The result is a person who's also clean on the outside.

> When Jesus had finished speaking, a Pharisee invited him to
> eat with him; so he went in and reclined at the table. But the
> Pharisee, noticing that Jesus did not first wash before the meal,
> was surprised.
>   Then the Lord said to him, "Now then, you Pharisees
> clean the outside of the cup and dish, but inside you are full of
> greed and wickedness. You foolish people!" (Luke 11:37-40)

Jesus made clear, "You guys are full of greed and wickedness, but you clean the outside of the cup and think that's what God really expects. Wrong! What He wants is cleansing on the inside, an impartation of His character and wisdom in you. You are majoring on minors and minoring on majors and missing the heart of God."

We might also call this part of the plan, "keep the main thing the main thing."

4. Worship the Living God

Finally, if you want to be a wise person, *take every opportunity to worship God.*

What does wisdom have to do with worship? Everything. We were created to worship God. He loves hearing from us—as a husband loves hearing how much his wife adores him. (If you're a guy, you know all about that, right?) God loves for us to think about Him, praise Him, thank Him, and celebrate Him.

This is what Paul wrote in another letter. Note the results of having "foolish hearts" :

> The wrath of God is being revealed from heaven against all
> the godlessness and wickedness of men who suppress the truth
> by their wickedness, since what may be known about God is
> plain to them, because God has made it plain to them. For
> since the creation of the world God's invisible qualities—his
> eternal power and divine nature—have been clearly seen,
> being understood from what has been made, so that men are
> without excuse.
>
> For although they knew God, they neither glorified him as
> God nor gave thanks to Him, but their thinking became futile
> and their foolish hearts were darkened. (Romans 1:18-21)

Think of it this way: Glorifying God is the opposite of foolishness. People who are so caught up with themselves and their lives are too arrogant to stop and give thanks to God. They may see the works of God all around them, but they are too foolish to acknowledge that the Creator-King is at work. That's ridiculous. It's absurd. It's a foolish mistake we need to avoid.

God is worthy. He's wonderful. He spoke the universe into being, revealed Himself to the people of Israel, walked among humans in the person of Jesus, died, and rose from the dead. And He did it all for us. I mean, if that doesn't make us want to glorify Him, smile at Him, and sing to Him…well, then we have a serious problem.

Worshiping God is one of our most fundamental practices for obtaining wisdom. In Psalm 73 we find the psalmist struggling to cope with the injustices of our earthly existence. He grumbles about the prosperity of the wicked and the arrogance of the ungodly. He describes how envious he has become of their carefree ways and dishonest wealth. In verse 13 he becomes brutally honest, and then something happens:

> Surely in vain have I kept my heart pure;
>> in vain have I washed my hands in innocence.
> All day long I have been plagued;
>> I have been punished every morning.
> If I had said, "I will speak thus,"
>> I would have betrayed your children.
> When I tried to understand all this,
>> it was oppressive to me
> till I entered the sanctuary of God;
>> then I understood their final destiny. (verses 13-17)

Many worshipers today enjoy the music and experience of worship without the profound transformation that God desires. They have excitement and emotional involvement without understanding or obedience. Worship becomes an empty ritual that tickles their senses and pacifies their desire for a "God fix."

King David had just such an experience when he was bringing the ark into Jerusalem. If you follow the story in 1 Chronicles 13–15, you will find two joyous celebrations, two great processionals escorting the ark of the covenant into the great city. David, the newly established king of Israel, was leading both processions in worship, ushering the ark back into the center of Israelite culture and consciousness.

The first procession ended in disaster. Tragedy struck when Uzzah reached out his hand to steady the ark as it rode on a newly constructed cart. The second procession ended with David shedding his royal garments in the sight of all Israel in a humble demonstration of gratitude. Two scenes filled with passionate expression. One ended in grief, and the other ended in exuberant joy. The difference? Wisdom has been discovered, and obedience embraced.

We must understand that the bottom line of worship is lordship. The question is, does our worship have the application of wisdom? Do we make Christ Lord with our obedience?

Glorifying and worshiping God is always a very wise thing to do. Give yourself to Him with all of your heart, soul, mind, and strength. Never stop letting Him know how much you enjoy Him.

Are you still asking, "Ted, how does this really work? Where do I get the final kick of motivation to be wise and avoid foolishness?" Here's how:

> If any of you lacks wisdom, he should ask God, who gives
> generously to all without finding fault, and it will be given
> to him. But when he asks, he must believe and not doubt,
> because he who doubts is like a wave of the sea, blown and
> tossed by the wind. That man should not think he will receive
> anything from the Lord; he is a double-minded man, unstable
> in all he does. (James 1:5-8)

So, in other words, make it your goal to gain wisdom and be foolish no more!

Questions for Pastor Ted

Why is it that we sometimes look at foolish qualities in children as "cute"? When we tell stories of our childhood, we always seem to tell about the times we were "ornery." I suppose these stories are a lot more entertaining than stories about the times we obeyed. So I wonder if we're naturally drawn to foolishness. Isn't there something admirable about "simple" fools?

All children are fools. I know that sounds harsh, but that is why children need parents, extended family members, and a community to grow up in. Those who say children are wonderful, innocent beings who should rule the world have never been to a day-care center! Children are selfish and violent. We think their misbehavior is "cute" only because they are small. If they were the size or age of an adult, we would put them in a hospital or prison to protect others.

Does this seem too severe? Yes, probably so. Let me modify it some: When Jesus said to let the little children come to Him, He was referring to the innocence of children, and, of course, we all love and appreciate that innocence. We need to incorporate it into our own hearts. But as children grow, they must mature, respond to external restraints, and develop internal restraints. All kids must transition from dependence to independence and then to the wisdom of interdependence. At that point they have what it takes to be contributing members of a family, church, and community. When we're adults, foolishness is no longer cute. It's just foolish. So let children be children, and let adults be adults. Grow from foolishness to wisdom, and we'll all be relieved!

I'm in my forties and have made many foolish mistakes in my life. Is it possible for me to overcome the law of sowing and reaping so that I can live well and claim the benefits of wisdom from now on?

Start sowing good seed today. Everything you think, say, and do is a seed. So start now praying through the lists in the Bible that describe the goodness of God, and pray that those characteristics will be manifested in your life. Here are some Scriptures to use:

- *Isaiah 11:2-3:* "The Spirit of the LORD will rest on him—the Spirit of wisdom and of understanding, the Spirit of counsel and of power, the Spirit of knowledge and of the fear of the LORD—and he will delight in the fear of the LORD."

- *1 Corinthians 12:8-10:* "To one there is given through the Spirit the message of wisdom, to another the message of knowledge by means of the same Spirit, to another faith by the same Spirit, to another gifts of healing by that one Spirit, to another miraculous powers, to another prophecy, to another distinguishing between spirits, to another speaking in different kinds of tongues, and to still another the interpretation of tongues."

- *Galatians 5:22-23:* "But the fruit of the Spirit is love, joy, peace, patience, kindness, goodness, faithfulness, gentleness and self-control. Against such things there is no law."

As you begin to pray that God will give you these things, it will impact your thinking. For example, when you pray for knowledge, you'll probably lose some of the enjoyment you experience watching junky television shows, and you'll want to read more good books or maybe take a class on some topic that interests you. When you pray for the gift of prophecy, you'll become more aware of how to speak the way God would have you speak. With tongues and interpretation, you'll become aware of the necessity to pray the way God wants you to pray and to understand the impact of your prayers. Wisdom, of course, will serve every area of your life. Patience will contribute greatly to success. Each of these and many others from the Bible's lists of spiritual gifts and fruit will help you think, speak, and act the way God does.

As a result, your words will be more precise and honorable. And, of course, with accompanying actions that honor God and others, you are sowing seeds that will produce positive results in your future.

Now about your past: Some of the bad seeds you have sown will mature and impact your future, but not all of them. So from this point forward, sow good seed, be a person of God, and live an honorable life no matter what happens to you. As a result, you will finish well.

Nine

TAKE THE BLESSINGS...AND BLESS

D o you have any idea who you are?

Sure, you know your name, the family you came from, where you were born. But it's possible, even though you have known Christ for years, that there is still some confusion about your importance to God.

My friend, you are a child of Abraham. And that is a really, really big deal.

In the region of Galatia, most of the believers were Gentiles, so most likely they didn't know Abraham from Chuck. Back then if you weren't a Jew, the fact that almighty God had stayed intimately involved with the Jewish people for centuries didn't mean much to you. That's why Paul, when trying to convince the Galatians of their foolishness, had to do something like a PowerPoint presentation on topics such as God's covenant with Abraham to make his case. Here's one thing he told the Galatians: "Understand, then, that *those who believe* are children of Abraham" (Galatians 3:7, emphasis added).

This point was so important to Paul's argument because it was known that the Jewish people claimed they had an inside track to incredible blessings from God. That certainly was true; God had promised them much because they were His chosen people. But Paul, staying true to his revolutionary bent, stated boldly that the Jews were not exclusively chosen.

The Jews responded, in effect, "Hey, wait a minute! We are the descendants of Abraham—his seed—so what God promised Abraham is ours."

"No, sorry to rain on your parade," Paul responded, "but that's not accurate. Everything promised to Abraham was intended for *everyone* who believes. The blessings are not just for those who are biological descendants; they're for people who are believers in the covenant of Abraham and in the Lord Jesus Christ."

Whoa! Turn off the television. Put down your magazine. Let go of your mouse. This is incredibly important, not just a heartwarming human-interest story tagged on to the daily news. This news is coming to you from the throne of God. This will change your life if you get it. I'll repeat again what Paul said: "Understand, then, that those who believe are children of Abraham" (verse 7).

So if you believe that Jesus Christ is the Son of the living God, congratulations! Welcome to a remarkable family! Your spiritual father's name is Abraham. Put that on your business card.

Paul went on to say:

The Scripture foresaw that God would justify the Gentiles
by faith, and announced the gospel in advance to Abraham:
"All nations will be blessed through you." So those who have
faith are blessed along with Abraham, the man of faith.
(verses 8-9)

Did you catch what he said there? Everybody who has faith is blessed along with Abraham, the man of faith.

Look at verse 14: "He redeemed us in order that the blessing given to Abraham might come to the Gentiles through Christ Jesus, so that by faith we might receive the promise of the Spirit."

If you believe in Jesus and have accepted His sacrifice and life for you, *it does not matter if you are a Jew or a Gentile.* All you need to do is page back to the book of Genesis, make a list of the blessings God promised to Abraham, and claim them for yourself—tuck that list in your pocket.

The phrase "so that by faith we might receive the promise of the Spirit"—oh, man, you better get a good grip; this is going to be some kind of ride!—means that all the favor from God, all the spiritual gifts, all the power available because of what God did with Abraham is available to you and to me. Break out the popcorn, peanuts, and Cracker Jack candy! Put on the paper hats and blow up the balloons. It's time to party. I mean, with this kind of news, how could any Christian ever stop smiling?

A few lines later in his letter, Paul clarified that even though God gave the Law to Moses more than four hundred years after His covenant with Abraham, the Law did not supersede the Abrahamic promise (see verses 16-17). The promise to Abraham's "seed" was actually a promise to Christ—and for all those who would later believe in Him.

Because Paul said those things, we can understand why he was perceived as such a radical, particularly by the Jews. Here's how he explained it:

> For if the inheritance depends on the law, then it no longer
> depends on a promise; but God in his grace gave it to Abra-
> ham through a promise. (verse 18)

If some of this information is making your eyes glaze over—the way mine do when I hear a word like *calculus*—please hang with me. You must get this! We are unpacking Paul here, and often people think his ideas are just too deep and complicated for us commoners to grasp. Forget that! What he is saying here is very clear and easy to understand. You must accept how much God favors you, loves you, and wants to do mighty deeds in your life. If you do not realize that everything God said to Abraham applies to you, you'll read Abraham's story as history, a moldy tale that applies only to other people in some distant time and place. That's not true! Every bit of it applies to you, which is what Paul is trying to pound into the heads of his "foolish" Galatian pals.

Let me say it again: *All the favor God expressed toward Abraham is expressed to you right now when you receive it by faith.*

I can almost hear the wheels turning—tortured thoughts seeking to beat the truth to a pulp: *I am just not good enough for God to really favor me.*

Perhaps, but it's your faith in Jesus that makes you good enough, or at least valuable enough.

Arrrrggghhhh, this just can't be true! Do you know how weak my prayer life is?

No, stop it! You will become stronger in prayer by accepting the fact that God favors you, loves you, and wants to do miracles in your life. God is a benevolent God who wants to deliver His life and blessing to your heart. His desire is to do profound things in each of us, but we must receive His involvement by faith.

Here's a True or False quiz that echoes the questions Paul asked the Galatians. How would you respond to these statements?

- I received my salvation because I was good enough.
- I received the Spirit because I was good enough.

- I received a miracle because I was good enough.
- I experienced healing because I was good enough.

The answers? False, false, false, and false!

Every one of us was saved, filled with the Spirit, healed, given a great prayer life, and everything else simply by faith in the Lord Jesus Christ.

THE PROMISES

Let's review some of the specifics of what God promised to Abraham. Keep in mind that what God said to Abraham is intended for *your* life and mine:

> The LORD had said to Abram, "Leave your country, your people and your father's household and go to the land I will show you." (Genesis 12:1)

Based on this verse alone, you can go into your prayer closet knowing that God loves you and will lead you to blessings in your life. Wherever your "there" is, you don't have to stay there. (Whatever happened to the English teachers who would rap your hand with a ruler for writing a sentence like that? Where's my editor when I need him?)

God wants you to leave some things behind. Where are you living? I don't mean your house. I'm talking about your habits and attitudes, maybe some rotten character qualities. You don't have to stay there. You don't need to hang out in a landfill, beat up and discouraged all the time. By faith—because you are a child of Abraham—you may say boldly, "I am a man of God! (or I am a woman of God!) I can blow this joint in Jesus's name."

This is why you don't need to be addicted to drugs, alcohol, or pornography. You don't have to have a foul mouth or abuse the people you love. You don't have to gossip or overeat. You don't have to get a divorce, betray your business partner, or cheat on your taxes. You have no obligation to fail in life just because your dad said you were no good or a teacher said you were stupid. You are not obligated to be a loser! Isn't it great you can live a life of freedom, victory, might, power, and authority in Christ Jesus your Lord? Talk about *good news!*

An extension of the meaning of God's request to Abraham is that each of us may also need to leave the security of what we are comfortable with in order to follow the Lord. We need to get out of Dodge—to saddle up and ride. If you, like everyone else, are living an "I'm getting by" life, punching the clock, getting some stuff done, and watching some reality-TV shows; if you are living without drive, not teaming up with what the Spirit of the Lord is doing and not connected dynamically with a church, then God is saying to you, "Come on, break out of that! Get moving." He may not mean that literally, but He certainly means it *spiritually.* We have to be willing to break free from the limitations of our pasts and become everything God wants us to become.

And there's more. Here's what Genesis 12 says:

> I will make you into a great nation
>   and I will bless you;
> I will make your name great,
>   and you will be a blessing. (verse 2)

Did you take note of what God says twice about blessing? "I will bless you" and "You will be a blessing." In other words, when you are at prayer, you don't have to say, "Oh, God, *p-l-e-e-a-a-s-s-e* find a way to bless me; *please* help me; oh, *please,* I need Your attention." You don't have to do that! Just open your hands and confidently say,

Oh, Father, I thank You that Your blessing is on my life. I thank You that You have created me to be a blessing to other people. I thank You that You have done a miracle in me, Lord God, so that I can love, give, and take care of other people. So that I can encourage and strengthen them because Your blessing is on my life!

When God says, "I will make you into a great nation," that means there's a blessing on your children and your spiritual children—the people who are in your sphere of influence. Sometimes people shy away from being a righteous influence over others. Don't you be afraid! Let God bring people into your life whom you can coach how to receive His blessings and spread His glory on the earth.

In addition to "doing the Word together," this is another reason why I am such a believer in small groups in the church. Groups provide a natural, nonthreatening opportunity for people to coach others. God wants to bless you so that you can serve and bless others. He wants to bless you so that He can pour out His Spirit in you and expand your sphere of influence. He is saying, "I will make you into a great nation! Not a wimpy nation, a loser nation, or a spineless nation, but a *great* nation!"

Look at God's vision for your realm of influence:

The LORD said to Abram after Lot had parted from him, "Lift up your eyes from where you are and look north and south, east and west. All the land that you see I will give to you and your offspring forever. I will make your offspring like the dust of the earth, so that if anyone could count the dust, then your offspring could be counted. Go, walk through the length and breadth of the land, for I am giving it to you." (Genesis 13:14-17)

If you are in partnership with Jesus, you are intended to make a lasting impact on the world. That's just what Abraham's offspring *do*.

But, of course, our enemy, Satan, wants none of this. He, as well as our sinful natures and the world, comes at us and plants doubts that can beat us down and leave us mumbling, "Well, I just thank God I'm saved by the skin of my teeth. But nobody should expect much out of me. *Sigh.*"

Come on, now, you are not saved by the skin of your teeth! You are saved by the blood of the Lord Jesus Christ, which means you are thoroughly and completely saved—*one hundred percent*. You are an heir of Abraham. You have the promises of God on your résumé. God is for you, and if God is for you, who in the world can be against you? Unless you don't believe the Bible.

Only people who really don't believe the Bible walk around saying, "I don't know; I just hope to influence at least one person in my lifetime. Maybe God will grant me enough grace, but I am just a wicked, awful sinner." Yes, wicked, awful sinners do need to be forgiven, delivered, and healed in Jesus's name. But no one has to be controlled by all that bad stuff. We all can rise up and fly—be the people God wants us to be.

The doubters may say, "Oh, that sounds kind of arrogant—to think God has that much interest in just any old person!"

On the contrary. It is arrogant to think that you have a better plan than what the Word of God teaches—and yet you end up failing over and over again. Sin makes you selfish and overly self-conscious. It makes you obsessively concerned about me, mine, ours—what everybody thinks of me. When you get delivered of that stuff and understand God's blessing on your life, then instead of focusing on yourself, you start thinking, *Man, what am I going to do with God's blessing in my life so that I can serve others?* You become so enthusiastic that you will pray, *I thank You, Lord Jesus, for the people You've given me to influence. I thank You that You are making me a great nation. Thank You that Your blessing is on my life.*

A GREAT NAME

Now I want to explain another blessing of being named in Abraham's will. This is particularly meaningful to me because I am not what you would describe as a polished or politically correct type of person. When God's blessing is on your life, He covers for some of your mistakes, such as saying the wrong thing at the wrong time—a "gift" I use many days. But because God's blessing is on my life, I can keep asking for forgiveness and continue to accomplish good things.

I remember a time I returned from an international trip. I was in a jet-lagged bad mood for about three days, during which I fought with every person I talked to on the phone. I'm not saying I had a right to act like that. I hate sinning because it takes so much time and energy to go back and clean up all the messes. This time I had to write a whole bunch of apology notes. But here's the amazing thing: Even when I'm clanking along, I know God's blessing is on me. When we sometimes say the wrong things, do the wrong things, go the wrong direction, or whatever, God's blessing remains on us.

Our model for this is none other than our dad, Abraham. Do you remember some of his escapades—like that Hagar incident and those embarrassing situations when he hid behind Sarah's skirts, posing as her brother? You get the picture.

But the Lord promised Abraham, "I will make your name great" (Genesis 12:2).

A good name is worth a lot—more than "great riches," the Bible says (Proverbs 22:1). The opposite is true too. Some people have names that are mud. When people think of John or Sally, the thoughts that come to mind are, *He's a liar! She's a gossip.* Or you hear a person's name and think of mistrust or dishonor. But when you think of other people, you think of honor, dignity, power, and life. Or you may recall their great deeds of sacrifice or service. Some people are known for being mighty in the Spirit's power, in evangelism, or in missions. A name really does mean something.

Do you want your name to stand for mediocrity or greatness? If you will cooperate with Him, God will make your name great. It's a promise.

I don't know about you, but I want to accomplish everything I can for the kingdom of God. I want to see it expand. So I want to pray and be a powerhouse of the Holy Spirit's activity. I don't want to be timid or shy. I don't want the power of sin and darkness to rule over me. I have no obligation to fail. I have no obligation to be ineffective in ministry in America, Tibet, or anywhere in the world, because God has created His children to go everywhere—to reach all the nations of the earth.

I want to encourage you, no matter where your life takes you on a daily basis, to always be a blessing. As you interact with your spouse, take the kids to school, or go to work, keep saying to yourself, "I'm going to be a blessing to people."

Why do we want to do this? To not do it would be to deny who we are! It's in our spiritual genetic code to bless others—we are like Abraham. We are blessed so we can bless others. So we want to be a blessing to a teenage girl who got into trouble and has an unwanted pregnancy. We want to bless a lonely, angry junior-high boy and pull the cigarette out of his mouth and take the gun out of his hand. He needs to be filled up with God and have his life changed before he starts shooting at somebody.

God has commissioned us to be a blessing to everyone on the earth. That's why we love being a blessing to other people! We love giving. We love being kind, thoughtful, and faithful. We love being gentle with others. We love sending kids to camp and joining a march for the unborn. That's also why we pray over the nations and cry out to God for the gospel to reach unreached people groups. That's why we give our money to mission efforts near and far away.

It won't always be easy, but as you bless others, God will bless you. Doesn't this make sense? So why doesn't the river within us flow out of us more of the time?

I think I know why. We are deluded in our thinking. We act more as if we are descendants of Joe, not Abraham. We are convinced we need to be self-consumed, to concentrate on taking care of me, mine, and ours. We forget or ignore the truth that God has created us to be the seed of Abraham. God has created us to impact other people in significant ways, to leave home and go next door or to the far reaches of the world and make an impact—not necessarily or always with our physical presence, but certainly with our giving, our prayers, our intentional love for others. This is our covenant, and it's an incredible gift and opportunity.

There is no retreat; there is no turning back; there is no cowering before the forces of darkness. Our charge is clear, and we have the blessing of God to help us—unless we allow sin to pollute our hearts, making us proud, selfish, judgmental, angry, bitter, self-conscious, self-righteous, mean, and all those kinds of things.

Listen, shake off that old stuff, rise up in Jesus's name, open your hands in your prayer closet, and say,

> In the name of Jesus, I put to death my old sin nature, and I open my life up to all the gifts and the fruit of the Holy Spirit. I am of the seed of Abraham, because I am in Christ and Christ is in me. And because I am of the seed of Abraham, the blessing of the Lord God Almighty is on my life. The favor of God is on my life. O God, I thank You for that!
>
> Thank you for sins forgiven, for a clean conscience, for no obligation to sin, for no obligation to fail. Instead, I have the freedom to join with brothers and sisters and take the land to the north, the south, the east, and the west.
>
> Father, I thank You that Your blessing is on my life. I thank You that You've created me to be a recipient of Your blessing and to be a blessing to others. Lord, You are doing a miracle in my life. Oh, thank You that You like me! Thank You that by faith in the Lord Jesus Christ, You've given me a dream and a vision. My name can stand for something that brings honor to Your name. O God, I give You praise and honor.
>
> Because of all that, Lord, I want to be a blessing. I want to

love. I want to give. I want to serve. I want to pray. I thank You for the privilege of loving, giving, serving, and praying.

Devil, you can't stop me now! I have the gift of God and am full of Him. O God, I give You glory!

Now, go for it! Accept your place. Claim your name. Find your courage. Go into your world—the whole world. Take your blessings and bless others.

Questions for Pastor Ted

How do we know specifically what spiritual gifts God has for us as individuals? For example, are we all called to be teachers or prophets or intercessors? Is this a name-it-and-claim-it thing?

You don't have to guess what you are called to do. For starters, there are tests you can take to help you identify your spiritual gifts and your role in the body of Christ. In addition, you can talk with your good friends about it and see what they think. Tell them that it won't be helpful if they say nice things to you that are not true. I know some people who should be Sunday-school teachers but think they are prophets because their friends don't have the heart to tell them otherwise. Whew. What a mess! They would do more for the body if they had a better picture of what they are really gifted at doing. Our friends want us to be great, which is wonderful, but we all need realistic help. Find the tests, talk with your friends, encourage them to tell the truth, and then serve faithfully in the small things.

As I try to be a blessing and serve others, I tend to overextend myself. When I try to set boundaries, I feel as if I'm using them as an excuse not to serve. How do you strike a balance in this area?

Age and experience. This process is natural for everyone who wants to serve, especially if you have talents others would like to utilize. Think about high-school track: Find your pace and keep it. Otherwise you won't finish the race.

Ten

LOVE IS A BIG DEAL

The apostle Paul would have really loved Viola Binder—just like I really love her. Knowing and serving people like Viola is what following Jesus is all about.

Viola Binder is a longtime member of New Life Church. When she is healthy enough, I can depend on her being in the same chair every Sunday morning, praying for others and me.

Viola has quite a story. She was married to a much older former Nazi SS trooper named Fritz, a really tough, foul guy who had only one leg. But Viola loved him, and to help make ends meet for the family, Viola would rise early, put on a miner's hat—with light—and crawl on her hands and knees up and down the median of Nevada Boulevard in Colorado Springs, collecting the worms that would surface when the sprinklers came on. Later in the morning she would sell the worms to fishermen to get enough money to buy some food for Fritz and herself and maybe pay a bill or two.

Life had not been easy for Viola, and when she showed up at New Life, she had a lot of needs. Over time the church was able to help her with some dental work, new clothes, classes at a community college, and other things. God blessed her, and when she got on her feet financially and otherwise, she turned around and helped others. Above all, she became an incredible prayer warrior.

One day Gayle and I came home, and there was Viola on her hands and knees scrubbing our garage floor with soap and water.

"Viola, what are you doing?" I asked.

"I am determined to find a way to show you and Gayle how much I love you," she said. As you already know, she didn't have much money or other resources. But she was full of Christ's love. So there she was scrubbing our garage floor—at least that was something she could do. As a young man still in my twenties, it would never have occurred to me to scrub my own garage floor, much less anyone else's! But Viola had seen how dirty it was and knew that Gayle and I had our hands full with other things. It was a little embarrassing, but it felt good.

Because of this incident and too many others to count, I can tell you for sure that Viola loves us.

As the years have passed, Viola's health has failed. Sometimes when she's at home sick in bed, she will call my assistant at the office and say, "Meg, tell Pastor Ted, I know he's busy, I don't want to bother him, but you tell him I prayed for him for four hours today."

To be honest, there have been times when I'm not sure I could have preached another sermon without Viola's prayers. The spiritual progress of our church has been fueled by the prayers of Viola and others like her. Regardless of how large or successful New Life becomes, I will always say, "I don't know if we could have done this without Viola." Her kind of love builds the body of Christ.

When Paul wrote, "I plead with you, brothers" (Galatians 4:12) near the end of his letter to the believers in Galatia, he was saying,

"Look, I've laid out the argument here for the gospel. Now, if you will listen to me for no other reason, do not forget how much we are bound to one another by love. Do you realize how deeply and desperately we are in love with one another? This is so important. Don't let these guys who came from Jerusalem mess this up. Don't buy into this foolishness. Don't let them bewitch you. Don't let them steal your joy. Don't let them take your innocence and turn you into old, grumbling sourpusses. Instead, flow in the divine nature of your loving God!"

THE REAL BODY OF CHRIST

If love is what defines us as Christians, then what defines a church? The core of a church does not consist of its programs, music, sermons, or structure. There's nothing wrong with any of those elements, and every good church has them. But when you boil everything down, the church is a place where we love and take care of one another.

Here's another Haggardism for the collection: *The real body of Christ happens when hearts connect and love flows among them.*

I was raised on a farm in Indiana with six siblings and wonderful Presbyterian parents. We kids never heard a harsh word between Mom and Dad, and we never doubted the security of their relationship. In the small town of six thousand people that we grew up in, there was never a threat of violence or theft, because everyone knew everyone else. When we went to the grocery story, we knew the owner, the workers, the checkout clerks, and the baggers who helped Mom get the groceries to the car. People helped people. There was a lot of love in our town, but it wasn't an ooey-gooey, mushy-fuzzy, marshmallowy type of love. Instead, it was tangible. People didn't say,

"I love you" very often, but they performed daily actions that expressed their love.

As a result of these boyhood experiences, I don't believe love is exclusively a feeling or something that is merely expressed verbally. Although it's nice to hear people say they love one another, very often these are empty words. Feelings and words are nice, but love expresses itself in actions. It's observable, verifiable, and substantive. You can see love. You can experience love. It's tangible.

So what is love? I know there are various definitions describing different aspects of love, and we will discuss some of them in the next chapter. But for this discussion, the common definition I use is this: *Love is caring enough about another person to live for his or her good.*

God is love. He's living for our good.

A father loves his children. He's living for their good.

A husband loves his wife. He's living for her good.

Love is an intentional decision to care enough about others to make their lives better. It doesn't happen by accident. It happens because it is premeditated and planned. Love is when one person determines to act a certain way on behalf of another.

For God so loved the world that he gave his one and only Son,
that whoever believes in him shall not perish but have eternal
life. (John 3:16)

God doesn't just feel love for people, nor does He just tell us about it. He did something about it. What He did was planned and observable, and it produced a tangible result. People who have not received the benefits of His love can observe others receiving it. Romans 5:8 says, "But God *demonstrates* his own love for us in this:

While we were still sinners, Christ died for us" (emphasis added). Love is a demonstration.

With this in mind, think about the 1 Corinthians 13 definition of love:

> Love is patient, love is kind. It does not envy, it does not boast, it is not proud. It is not rude, it is not self-seeking, it is not easily angered, it keeps no record of wrongs. Love does not delight in evil but rejoices with the truth. It always protects, always trusts, always hopes, always perseveres.
>
> Love never fails. (verses 4-8)

One of my favorite phrases from that passage is "always protects." When we love one another, we provide incredible safety and security for one another. If a woman loves a friend, she will defend her. If a man loves his family, he will take action to ensure that his wife and children have shelter. Jesus certainly did this. "This is how we know what love is: Jesus Christ laid down his life for us. And we ought to lay down our lives for our brothers" (1 John 3:16). Love is all about what we can do to protect the ones we love.

Love is also helpful. If we love others, we strengthen them. If a need exists, we do what we can to help the other person, regardless of the cost or consequence to ourselves.

So, being the practical guy I am, I have to ask myself, "Can love be measured?" The answer: Absolutely! Think about it. You can put love on a scale of 1 to 10 and measure it. Is your church a 7? Is your home a 4? Is your marriage a 9?

It's a wonderful exercise to ask, "How loving am I?" On a scale of 1 to 10, how loving have you been to the following people?

- spouse
- parents
- family
- close friends
- pastor
- church members
- school or work associates
- neighbors

Interestingly, you can measure it, and then you can think and pray about it and raise the love level in your home, church, and marriage. Paul said in 1 Thessalonians 3:12, "May the Lord make your love increase and overflow for each other…just as ours does for you." It's not that hard. People like Viola know how to raise the love level, which is important, because Jesus said, "By this all men will know that you are my disciples, if you love one another" (John 13:35).

We can take the same list of people and measure the love they express toward us. It's also meaningful to measure on a scale of 1 to 10 how easy or hard it is for you to say "I love you" to them and really mean it.

As a pastor, I want people in the church I serve to really know and love one another. I want them to know how to increase the level of love in their lives. I want them to know one another's names, where others live, and what's really going on in their lives. I want them to have meals together, to help raise each other's kids, to be at the weddings of each other's kids. I want them to pray for one another and to go through life's struggles shoulder to shoulder. And finally, I want them to grow old and get wrinkly together. If people stick together in the body of Christ, we won't end up having funerals with nobody there to say good-bye.

As hard as this is to believe, there are some people who don't like me or my preaching, but they still come to New Life Church! They do it because they are connected in love to others there.

Love is our choice. And it's up to us to appropriate the love of God in our lives and develop the skill of loving others. This is why Jesus said,

> "Love the Lord your God with all your heart and with all your soul and with all your mind." This is the first and greatest commandment. And the second is like it: "Love your neighbor as yourself." All the Law and the Prophets hang on these two commandments. (Matthew 22:37-40)

So, was Jesus loving when He rebuked people? Yes. He was living for their good. And by commanding us to do the same, He revealed that our love would automatically fulfill all the commandments in Scripture. Jesus emphasized this idea when He said, "If you love me, you will obey what I command" (John 14:15).

People who love one another don't betray one another. As a result, where there is love, there is no immorality, no deceit, no stealing, no selfish ambition. It's easy to be honorable when you are living for the good of those around you.

Love is the key to a fulfilled life. If we don't know how to love, we might not be experiencing the nature and life of God the way we could. But don't despair. Love can be learned. How do I know this? Because loving others is a choice we make. When Jesus said, "Love your neighbor as yourself" (Matthew 19:19), He was asking us to do something we could choose to do. When He said, "But I tell you: Love your enemies and pray for those who persecute you" (Matthew

5:44), He was exhorting us to make a choice to do good. When He taught us about authentic friendship by saying, "Greater love has no one than this, that he lay down his life for his friends" (John 15:13), He was saying that love is not a feeling, and sometimes it is no fun. Instead, it is a sacrifice to make another person's life better.

In giving our lives away for others, we show our love. Love doesn't drop from the sky onto us, and it doesn't come and go with feelings. It's a conscious decision we make to improve the lives of those we choose to care about.

Our churches are to be bastions of love. Good feelings? Maybe. Helpful actions? Always. When you experience that kind of love, you can endure a lot.

In case you are missing this, let me emphasize that *love is a big, big deal.*

We make love our goal at New Life Church, and this begins with our pastoral staff. I really love these folks—and they really love me. I'm not kidding! We really enjoy one another. We are a team in life and ministry, and we seek to help one another and make one another's lives better.

This love trickles down to the whole church, because everyone on our staff influences—loves—a large number of people in the church. It's our worldview to genuinely connect with and love the body of Christ. We don't just "talk" about love, nor do we criticize the body of Christ for its lack of love. (Remember: Jesus is the Head of the body, and I think He is doing a great job!) Instead, we *do* it; we genuinely love each other.

Too many churches and Christian ministries spend too much time having to manage carnal power and feelings. Instead of all the fighting over power, money, and position that goes on in too many churches, wouldn't it be fantastic to hear about a church in which the biggest problem was controlling all the love people had for one another? What if the people in such a church were almost overdosing on encouraging and adoring one another? Imagine if they were always sending one another money, cards, and food—and secretly paying each other's bills. Imagine if the people were doing so many nice things for one another and were so out of control with loving-kindness that church leaders had to hold a special business meeting to get everyone calmed down. Wouldn't you want to be in the middle of that?

When we talk about love, we are talking about what the late pastor John Osteen called the "divine flow." This is the love that flows from God into your heart as through a conduit, because you are loved unconditionally by Jesus.

Jesus accepts you, He loves to hear from you in prayer, and He loves to take care of you. As you experience His love, a divine flow will naturally occur in you toward other people. It's pure; it's honorable; it's wonderful. And when that divine flow happens between people, their hearts connect, and they often become partners in various endeavors throughout life. I have attended many conferences, classes, and seminars on different aspects of church life. Very seldom is the subject of love discussed. I think it's because most people assume that love is exclusively a feeling, or maybe they see love as an empty word because of negative past experiences. But I don't think we can move forward in the kingdom of God unless we experience love and increase the level of love around us.

If we want to follow God, we must learn to live by love.

God's love is pure, wholesome, giving, kind, supportive, forgiving, and constructive, which is why it's so important for us to open up every room in our lives and have them cleansed from sin. Those who are not cleansed have a difficult time being the conduit of God's love that He desires. Sinfulness allows the old sin nature and the world to pervert the divine flow of God's love into a sexual attraction or an emotion that might develop into codependent relationships or some strange controlling or manipulative spirituality. Obviously, authentic love requires wisdom that comes from God and needs to be inculcated into our lives through healthy family and church relationships. God's love is our marker, and the world's perversion of this love is our undoing.

You and I see all kinds of things in the world, but there is nothing more wonderful than people who love people. And I don't think there's any trust greater than the trust between people who are bonded together with an authentic bond of love. Woe to the man or woman who despises or just does not recognize such a sacred trust of love and misuses or abuses it.

Love is God's sacred trust to the world.

Many things are speculated or said about the apostle Paul, but one of them is beyond debate: He really loved people. Here in this letter to the deluded Galatians, as frustrated as he was with them, he continued to be so bonkers in love with them that he couldn't let go of them without a fight.

After presenting various arguments to convince the Galatians to stop being foolish, he cried out, "Become like me. You don't need to go the other direction; you need to be like me" (see Galatians 4:12).

One of the greatest evidences of love is living a life that others can emulate. We must never say, "Do what I say, not what I do." Stop it! Just do the right thing. You're a human being, able to be filled with the Holy Spirit and able to obey God's Word. So live the kind of life that can help others and will be an example for them to follow.

Every one of us should be able to say to others, "Go ahead. Handle your life the way I handle my life. Treat your spouse the way I treat mine. Pray the way I pray. Read your Bible the way I read mine. Manage your money the way I manage mine." This is biblical leadership and authentic love. When we intentionally live this way, life goes much more smoothly. Everybody needs models, so we have an opportunity to live in such a way that those around us know we're here for their benefit. We're living to serve them.

Modeling can happen in many ways in your life. One night I was standing in the kitchen kissing Gayle, and one of our sons, Elliott, came in and said, "Kissing again? Smooching again? Oh, my gosh, what am I going to do?" He's a dramatic little man! So I turned to him and said, "When you grow up, you love your wife the way I love mine. I love her, I adore her, I protect her. You do the same, young man." And then he ran up and hugged both of us and said, "Can I get in on this?"

Paul was not shy about urging others to mimic him. He had abandoned some of the traditions of his fathers to become free in Christ and reach the Gentiles. He knew that had been a good thing. He now urged others to follow in his steps.

Paul next reminded the Galatians of his condition when he first visited them: "As you know, it was because of an illness that I first preached the gospel to you" (verse 13).

Bible students have speculated for a long time as to just what Paul's thorn was. Frankly, nobody can really say for sure. Here are some of the educated guesses:

- persecution
- temptations of the flesh
- physical appearance (Apparently, Paul was not that good looking. He would have made a lousy televangelist!)
- violent headaches, maybe migraines
- eye trouble—partial blindness (This could explain why some of Paul's letters were written in large print, and why he often made use of a scribe.)
- epilepsy
- malaria (Paul had ministered in an area known then—and now—for malaria. So the theory is that he had contracted malaria and had perhaps gone to Galatia to find relief. Galatia was at a higher elevation, so the folk wisdom of Paul's era was that if you went there you could rid yourself of the headaches and other suffering that accompanies the disease.)

I think the malaria theory has more credibility than the others. The headache pain from malaria is horrible—like having a spike pounded into your skull—and it causes your eyes to throb. I've read that some people die from malaria, because, in trying to chase away the pain, they bang their heads on walls, bedstands, or other objects. Or they'll damage their own eyes trying to find relief from the awful aching.

Here's my insight: Paul was busy doing ministry and did not plan to go to Galatia, but somewhere he contracted malaria. He was advised to visit Galatia to get relief from the pain, and while there, he preached the gospel.

Even though my illness was a trial to you, you did not treat me with contempt or scorn. Instead, you welcomed me as if I were an angel of God, as if I were Christ Jesus himself. What has happened to all your joy? I can testify that, if you could have done so, you would have torn out your eyes and given them to me. (verses 14-15)

In the simplest terms, Paul was saying, "You loved me. It wasn't pretty or easy. But you connected. You took care of me. You loved me."

I've never asked her, but I think Viola Binder would joyfully give her eyes for Gayle or me. In fact I had malaria once, and Viola spent an afternoon on our front doorstep praying for me quietly so as not to disturb me. That's the kind of love the Galatian church had for Paul and Paul had for them.

Do you know that some people go all the way through life never having anybody really love them? And others never really love anybody else. Jesus came to show us how to love so that kind of thing would not happen! We were not created to live without love. We followers of Jesus need to be experts in how to love appropriately. We need to know what affection, affirmation, and admiration are. We need to know how to say to somebody, "I would more than happily give up my eyes so that you could see." That's the kind of love we have flowing inside us. It needs to get out to other people where it can do some good.

Next Paul gets more direct: "Have I now become your enemy by telling you the truth?" (verse 16).

Paul was clever with words, so he knew how to make them his sword when necessary. Here he took a jab at the Galatians he loved in order to cut to their hearts and make sure they really understood what he was saying.

How does that work for you? When you love someone, can you

tell him or her? If you really have affection and admiration for somebody, do you go ahead and say it? As I know so well, just because you show love does not mean that others will give you a loving response.

Love does involve risk. Remember the day in elementary school when you scribbled a note with a pencil and passed it along: "I love you. Do you love me? Check the box below. Yes or no." And you knew that by sending that note, you had lost control. The love of your life might just shriek and show the note to all her friends, causing laughter to thunder in your ears. And with it, that terrible feeling of rejection.

We've all suffered through similar experiences. That's why, too often, the note is never sent.

Well, when you link up with Christ in this way of living that overflows with love, you are on the playground all the time.

I meet people who don't have friends who love them or others to love in return, and they lead lonely, dry lives. They get mean and crusty. They're the ones honking and snarling at people in traffic.

Love anyway. In the name of the Lord Jesus, be brave—send the note and take the risk. The old saying is true: "It's better to have loved and lost than to have never loved at all."

LOVE MUST PREVAIL

Now Paul again goes after the enemies of the gospel:

Those people are zealous to win you over, but for no good. What they want is to alienate you from us, so that you may be zealous for them. It is fine to be zealous, provided the purpose

is good, and to be so always and not just when I am with you.
(Galatians 4:17-18)

Paul loved his Galatian protégés so much that he was willing to
engage in some conflict for the truth. He reminded his friends that
the people who were trying to talk them out of believing in the real
gospel were not motivated by a love like Paul's. They didn't care about
these people the way Paul did. He seemed to be saying, "They
wouldn't become like you! They wouldn't go to your house! They
wouldn't take care of your kids!" Paul was emphasizing how important personal relationships are: "You're mine, Galatians, foolish or not."

Christian faith is about love. There comes a time when love must
prevail, when it must really mean something and when it will cost us
something.

And then Paul wrote, "My dear children, for whom I am again in
the pains of childbirth until Christ is formed in you" (verse 19).

The phrase "dear children" misses something in the English trans-
lation. This is one of the more endearing things Paul could have said.
In the Greek it indicates "strong affection and adoration." He really
loved these guys. Although Paul obviously had never given birth to a
child, he knew what it was like to labor and to cry out in prayer to
God for the hearts of others.

The life we live in Christ is very interactive. It is somewhat mysterious, but God really wants to partner with us in His work. During
Creation, God had to do it all. But once He got men and women in
place on the earth, He gave them responsibilities and work. Nothing's
changed. We often wish that God would just zap people into the
kingdom. And then we wish He would zap them again to get them

perfectly sanctified. But that's not how it works. Much effort is normally required to bring about God's will here on earth. And it all starts with prayer—crying out to God for the birth of His life in us and others.

I've already told you how much love Viola Binder has shown for Gayle, me, and New Life Church. I'm glad I had the privilege one day to show Viola how much her church loves her.

When attendance at New Life reached about two hundred, a small buzz started around town, and three outstanding, well-to-do men and their wives showed up at our Sunday services. The three families attended church for several Sundays, after which the three men approached me and said cordially, "We really love how the church operates, your preaching style, and what you want to do in Colorado Springs. We would like to partner with you."

"Thank you so much," I said. "I appreciate that." These guys had prestige and a good reputation in the community. I was elated that they wanted to join with us. We needed all the help we could get.

These folks attended church for several months. Then one day we were sitting together and chatting, and one of the men said, "Pastor Ted, New Life Church has unlimited growth potential and can do some wonderful things. But in order for this church to reach its potential," and then he nodded over at Viola Binder, "you've got to find a way to get women like that off the front row."

I know people think that kind of thing all the time. In those days, Viola didn't always look so nice or wear the cleanest clothes. What got under my skin, though, was that these guys rudely said it out loud.

I replied, "Well, here's the deal, guys. Jesus said we are supposed to visit and help those who have need. Obviously, you have settled your issues in life, but Viola really needs us. So why don't you find a church where you can grow and be successful and do what you want to do. We're going to stick with Viola."

I don't recall seeing any of them at New Life again. I would have welcomed them. But they would have needed to understand that in the body of Christ everyone participates in the loving.

It's a big deal.

Questions for Pastor Ted

Is it possible to give someone grace just out of obedience to God? What if you don't feel gracious? Should I go through the motions anyway and hope that with time the Lord will change my heart so I'm not just putting on an act?

In our relationships, giving grace (favor) is a choice. It is good to choose to give grace, even when we don't feel like it. We don't want to be deceptive, but at the same time, we need to be disciplined. I tell people who don't like me that I would prefer they act as if they do rather than communicate hostility every time they see me. Isn't that civilized of me?

If you have hurtful feelings toward someone, make every effort to give grace to that person out of obedience to God, even if you don't feel it inwardly. You don't have to think of it as "an act" or "faking it." Just give grace. Giving grace often requires us to be merciful toward people who don't deserve it.

Sometimes people come up to me at church to ask my forgiveness for things they have said or done against me. When this happens, I stop them and ask if I know about what they've done. If they say no, I tell them that they need to repent and settle it with God, not me. If they were to tell me what they had said or done, then I'd be polluted and would have to deal with it. I would rather not know and instead let them work it out with God and whoever else is involved.

Why is it that some non-Christians seem to love more naturally and expansively than many believers?

Maybe they had better parents! Or maybe they do care more about others than we do. Or maybe they come from a culture that is more caring and kind than ours.

This is a great question for me to answer because I spent the early years of my life in Delphi, Indiana, a small farming community. When I lived there, the downtown stores didn't lock their doors, the cars were left unlocked with the keys in them, and any crime was managed by an "officer" who was really the city's part-time night watchman. Interestingly, though this community wasn't full of life-giving evangelical churches, it was dominated by Christian culture. People took care of one another. They authentically cared. As a result, even non-Christians were often more loving than are many Christians today.

We're paying for this right now in many ways in the body of Christ. Many of our Christian leaders love God and the Bible but don't seem to personally understand or know how to practice love. As a result, we must—let me emphasize *must*—be saturated in the love of Christ and apply it to our daily lives. Living without love is living without God. To say that we love God but don't love others is an illusion.

So what should we do? Commit to love ourselves and others now. How? Reject our own sin and serve others for the rest of our lives. Making others' lives better is our charge. What joy that gives us!

Eleven

PICK YOUR FRUIT

Too often when we talk about a topic like the fruit of the Spirit, we shift into spiritual autopilot. The fog rolls in, our eyes glaze over, our minds shut down. The material is so familiar that we think we can coast.

But I want you to be sure you understand something very clearly: Every moment of every day you are deciding what kind of fruit to pick from your personal orchard. Even just a moment ago. Even right now. You're picking fruit.

There, you just did it again.

As I have discussed often in this book, an invisible battle is going on inside you. Your beastly, sick, disgusting, obstinate sin nature is warring against the Spirit of God in you. This is not a friendly little wrestling romp in front of the fireplace in the family room. No, it's a vicious, no-holds-barred, take-no-prisoners battle. Vicious foes are trying to kill each other, and your life is at stake.

Someday, when the Lord Jesus returns or we experience physical death, each of us will get to leave our earthly body or "tent" and move on to the next dimension. That will end this daily battle, and in heaven we won't need to talk about the fruit of the Spirit. There we will just naturally be fruitful all the time.

But here it's another story. Now we don't always produce the fruit we need to. We plant the wrong seeds, produce the wrong harvest, often without noticing what we're doing. Frankly, many Christians—some who think they are delivering more delicious fruit than Pittman and Davis—produce more sour grapes than oranges. Yuck. Tastes bad!

I see this in myself, of course, but rather than give an illustration from my own life—that can be *so* embarrassing—let me show how this can look in someone else's life!

Once, after I had cut the grass at the house, I said to my youngest son, "Elliott, please get the broom and sweep the grass clippings off the sidewalk."

A breeze was blowing from the direction where he wanted to sweep. Elliott started brushing the grass clippings into the wind, and immediately they blew back into the area he had just swept. Now, rather than thinking, *I wonder if I could sweep* with *the wind,* Elliot lost his temper. He threw the broom down, stomped his foot, and burst into tears. "I am never sweeping again! You hate me!" he yelled at me.

At that moment he was not picking any fruit of the Spirit—some ripened patience, for example, would have been a good option for him. But he chose the opposite. He was very upset.

As his father, I decided to let him go through it. I preferred having him act like this as a young boy rather than when he's nineteen. So I stood there watching with my hands in my pockets. He was crying, sniffling, angry. And he wasn't done with me. "Why are you looking at me?" he screeched. He suspected I was thinking up a great pastor's lecture. Poor kid—he was right.

"Elliott, do you think there's a way you could figure out how to sweep this sidewalk without crying?"

"But the wind is blowing! Look at it! I can't do it!"

"If the wind is blowing this way," I said, "why don't you just sweep in the other direction, with the wind?" I grabbed the broom and showed him a few strokes. The grass departed as if by magic. He caught my brilliance immediately and laughed. He saw how ridiculously easy it was and did it himself. And that was the end of the tears and foot stomping.

This incident illustrates the choices we have: align ourselves with the Spirit and get into a good flow in life, or take the "I'll do it my way" approach. We all face these two paths constantly. With the Spirit we can go easy and steady, show some patience, and get the job done. But how many times have you and I done the equivalent of throwing down the broom and crying instead of allowing the Spirit of God to flow within us and produce a more positive, fruitful outcome?

Life doesn't have to be so hard.

So you and I have a decision to make: What or who is going to be in charge of our lives? Will it be the Holy Spirit, or will our old sin nature call the shots?

The choices we make reveal what's on the inside of us, which is why we need God's help to produce good fruit. He has to change us from within if we are to produce anything resembling good fruit. As Jesus said, "Make a tree good and its fruit will be good, or make a tree bad and its fruit will be bad, for a tree is recognized by its fruit" (Matthew 12:33).

What the world tries to do is let people stay bad at the core but look good on the outside. God's way makes more sense—just go ahead and transform people at their core so they "naturally" produce good fruit. It's easy. It's simple.

I don't believe that living the Christian life has to be either difficult or complex—at least most of the time. It requires some knowledge, which is why we have the Bible. It requires power, which is why we have the Holy Spirit. And it requires transformation, which is why we have healthy churches.

Continuing on in Matthew 12, Jesus developed this idea in His smooth, loving, always inoffensive style:

> You brood of vipers, how can you who are evil say anything good? For out of the overflow of the heart the mouth speaks. The good man brings good things out of the good stored up in him, and the evil man brings evil things out of the evil stored up in him. But I tell you that men will have to give account on the day of judgment for every careless word they have spoken. For by your words you will be acquitted, and by your words you will be condemned. (verses 34-37)

What was Jesus's deal? He was being so tough because He was speaking to the religious leaders. The Jewish teachers of the law were trying to get everybody to obey the rules, but this was impossible, because there was no power in the law to change the soul, the core of a person. It wasn't that the rules were inferior—don't commit adultery, don't lie, don't cheat, don't steal are great ideas. But people in their old sin nature are inherently, well, sinful. We just do all that bad stuff our moms warned us about.

The religious leaders claimed to be all about righteousness, but because these men had not dealt with their own sin nature, they were secretly breaking the rules themselves. Jesus had read their mail.

Every religious system produces hypocrites, because the only consistent answer to sin is the power of God operating inside a person.

The difference between Christianity and other religions is that Christians are transformed from the inside out. A Christian kills the old sin nature with the power of the Cross and then puts on Christ through the ministry of the Holy Spirit. It's the only way to go. You don't have to beat yourself or pray a certain way three times a day. You just have to receive the Spirit of God.

That's why Jesus lays the lumber to these guys. He says there is no way for human beings to control their tongues except by the power of the Holy Spirit. He drives the point home that you and I have this basic choice: to live life our own way or to surrender all and fill up with God's Spirit.

This is the same idea Paul emphasized later to the Galatians:

> So I say, live by the Spirit, and you will not gratify the desires
> of the sinful nature. For the sinful nature desires what is con-
> trary to the Spirit, and the Spirit what is contrary to the sinful
> nature. They are in conflict with each other, so that you do
> not do what you want. But if you are led by the Spirit, you
> are not under law. (5:16-18)

This is so very important. I urge you not to avoid or be afraid of the Holy Spirit. Don't be afraid to talk about the Holy Spirit, to dive into and dwell in the Spirit, to walk in the Spirit, to be transformed by the Spirit. Our Christian lives are futile without the Holy Spirit. We can't live the kind of life God wants us to live without Him.

I know you might be afraid of becoming too charismatic or becoming like a televangelist or a faith healer. Well, it's better to overcome your fears and obey Scripture than miss God's plan for your life. Be filled with the Spirit. Actually, Scripture urges more than that: It commands that we *continually* be filled with the Spirit. The best English translations actually should read, "Being continually filled with the Holy Spirit." So don't just be filled; instead, be *continually* filled.

When the Scriptures urge us to be "baptized in the Holy Spirit," it is clear that God recognizes our need to be immersed in the Holy Spirit. We can't be the people God wants us to be and avoid the ministry of the Holy Spirit. If we try to do this, we'll be like the religious leaders of Jesus's day: people with an appearance of godliness (which in our culture means people who are really nice) without the power of God (which means that the flaws in our lives are ever present, and we lack the demonstration of the Spirit's power in fullness).

My advice: Go to the mountaintop with a gallon of water, Scripture tapes, a tent, and some firewood, and stay there several days praying and fasting. While there, kill your old sin nature, soak in the Scriptures, and be filled with the Holy Spirit. Forgive others, repent of sin, soak in life, and go without food. Evaluate life. Think. Plan. But don't work. Leave your laptop and cell phone at home. After about three days of this, come back down the mountain and steadily continue being filled with His life through the Scriptures, the Spirit, and wholesome fellowship in the body. Go back to work, test what you've received, and in three or four months, you'll need to go to the mountaintop again.

This brief statement from the apostle Paul—"So I say, live by the Spirit" (verse 16)—contains the secret to your success. Even though avoiding it might still allow you to look good, at your core you'll not be your best. This is *the* truth that can keep you from ever becoming an alcoholic, a drug addict, or a spouse abuser. You do not need to ever bring shame to your name, family, or community. Really, the Christian life does not have to be that hard. All your strained attempts to be a good person will occur with less effort when you are filled with the Holy Spirit and are producing good fruit.

CHOOSE YOUR FRUIT

Most of us could get at least a C on a quiz that asked us to list the fruit of the Spirit. But how well would you do if I asked you to list the fruit of the flesh?

Since each of us is always deciding what kind of fruit we want to grow out of our lives, it makes sense to me that we should be experts at recognizing both good and bad fruit—sort of like knowing which mushrooms to pick in the forest.

This is how Paul described bad fruit:

> The acts of the sinful nature are obvious: sexual immorality, impurity and debauchery; idolatry and witchcraft; hatred, discord, jealousy, fits of rage, selfish ambition, dissensions, factions and envy; drunkenness, orgies, and the like. I warn you, as I did before, that those who live like this will not inherit the kingdom of God. (Galatians 5:19-21)

The fruit of the flesh is a disaster. These destructive attitudes and behaviors divide, hurt, wound, and destroy. They will mess up your marriage, bring discord into your family, and foul up your relationships in the church. You will spend money foolishly and wreck your health. You will be untrustworthy and cause people to dislike you.

You want devastation in your life? You don't have to pray and fast, study the Scriptures, or be filled with the Spirit to receive the acts of the sinful nature. They are already yours. It's also interesting, though, that if we go to church, tithe, have Christian friends, and work in a Christian ministry but aren't being filled with the Holy Spirit, these acts of the sinful nature are still ours. Neither a therapist, a pastor, a counselor, a Bible-study leader, nor a parent can get the acts of the sinful nature out of us. As good as these things can be, rote Scripture memorization or methodical prayer five times a day won't do it. There is only one way to overcome the acts of the sinful nature: Be filled with the Holy Spirit and plant a grove of fresh fruit.

Next, Paul draws the contrast and shows us what good fruit looks like:

> But the fruit of the Spirit is love, joy, peace, patience, kind-
> ness, goodness, faithfulness, gentleness and self-control.
> Against such things there is no law. (verses 22-23)

No law. Imagine that. There's no need for a law against these things because they represent the absolute best of human action and interaction.

Let's review quickly why Spirit fruit is so much to be preferred over flesh fruit. If we look at each piece closely, turn it over, smell it, taste it, have it for breakfast (okay, I'll stop), we'll be better equipped to produce it in our lives.

Love

Love is confusing for anybody who speaks the English language, because we use the word *love* for a variety of ideas. My definition for *love* is "caring enough about other people to live for their good." But for many, love can mean sexual attraction or brotherly affection. It can also describe the way a parent loves a child. It can mean how God gives Himself to us and how we respond. The same word can be used to mean everything from a divine, supernatural flow to a risqué experience, from how we feel about our spouses to how we feel about pizza and our favorite football team.

This confusion about love in English did not exist for the Greeks, however. The Greek language had four separate words to describe love. First was the word *eros*. Our English word *erotic* comes from this. It refers to sexual love between a man and woman. The second word was *philia*, the warm, affectionate love we feel for our best friends. Then there's *storge*, the love of parents and kids for each other. Finally, the word for supernatural love is *agape*, which is used in Paul's letter to the Galatians.

Agape is a Christian word. It was not a common word in the secular Greek literature of the biblical period. It means "unconquerable benevolence." With agape, it doesn't matter what another person may do that might insult, injure, or humiliate you. With agape love you always seek the highest good for that person. Human beings cannot have agape love on their own; that's why this is a Christian word. It describes a supernatural love. It's the love of the divine flow we mentioned earlier. It's what identifies Christians.

Joy

Much of the teaching on *joy* separates the meaning of the word from "happiness." That makes some sense because happiness tends to be contingent on external circumstances, while joy is a deep-seated, consistent hope that abides within a believer who's in relationship with Christ. Joy cannot be taken away, but happiness ebbs and flows, comes and goes.

Now sometimes when people talk about these words, they kind

of slam on happiness and build up joy. I say, why not go for both! We ought to have the deep roots of joy on the inside so that no matter what happens, we are okay. But we ought to live according to the principles of God so that our external world is in order and happy too.

Joy is incredible! It's more than optimism—it's hope, a surety that comes from trusting in God. Sometimes it looks reckless because it's just so deeply confident. It's a buoyancy that can come only from being in love with and trusting God. King David wrote,

> You turned my wailing into dancing;
>> you removed my sackcloth and clothed me with joy,
> that my heart may sing to you and not be silent.
>> O LORD my God, I will give you thanks forever.
>> (Psalm 30:11-12)

That's exactly what happens when we come into relationship with the Holy Spirit. When we're fellowshiping with God, we are transformed into creatures of joy.

Peace

Peace is a bigger idea than just freedom from trouble. Peace is tranquillity of heart, safety, security, assurance. Peace means "everything is all right both inside and outside"—it's having it all in order.

Some people live their whole lives and never know peace. They are born into families that are not in order, and they never know what healthy, wholesome relationships are like. However, anyone who obeys the Word of God and is filled to overflowing with the Holy Spirit can enjoy "the peace of God, which transcends all understanding" (Philippians 4:7). You can have peace in rush-hour traffic, in a courtroom, or in a waiting room at a hospital. You can have this incredible security that everything is all right and that you are safe.

Here's another Haggardism: *Peace is like living in a bubble.* It's like existing in an alternate reality, protected by a shield that guarantees your serenity. It's what non-Christians are looking for by drinking, getting stoned, and being immoral. Those experiences are impostors of peace. You can get as drunk as you want, but that will not bring you a peace that passes understanding. You can accumulate as much money as you want, but it's not going to give you satisfaction deep in your soul. You can become as famous as you want to be, but it's not going to give you a calm contentment. You need the fruit of peace.

Patience

Patience is not passivity; it's steady, humble persistence. I call it "persistence with birds singing." It's not stubbornness or bullheadedness. It's persistent endurance.

Think about the story of Job, one of the most misunderstood stories in the Bible. Job is often cited as an example of patience, and people advise one another to have the "patience of Job." But if you actually read the story, you'll wonder where that idea comes from. This guy doesn't seem too patient. He complains. He yells at his friends and God. He lists all his spiritual accomplishments and questions why the God he has served so faithfully would let all this bad stuff happen to him.

That doesn't look much like patience. But in a way it's a wonderful display of persistence with birds singing. Job complains, but he never—not once—rejects God. And when God comes on the scene and rebukes Job for being a hothead, Job humbly repents. He accepts God's discipline and accepts that his life belongs to God, and God can do with it what He pleases.

In other words, Job presses through. He gets upset, but he keeps the main thing the main thing. He hates his situation and wonders why it is happening, but he never transgresses into rejecting the ultimate authority of God. That's patience. It's a determination to get through.

I think one of the greatest secrets to living a successful Christian life is to simply stay steady. When you want to switch churches, spouses, careers, cities, houses, or cars, just stay steady. Don't move so fast. Wait six months without mentioning it to anyone. It's amazing how the cloud of strong emotions dissipates over time, and you can see more clearly to make a wise decision. If at all possible, I avoid making any major decisions when the pressure is on. Patience is a very good friend.

Patience is what people need when dealing with me. I was the youngest of four boys in my family (my two sisters came much later). Being the fourth born and the baby boy, I don't mind at all getting attention by tormenting others. Is tormenting a fruit of the Spirit? In my case, yes. Well…maybe. I know it brings me joy, and it's my way of helping others grow in patience.

Kindness and Goodness

I'm discussing the fruit of kindness and goodness together because the Greek word translated as "kindness" is sometimes translated as "goodness" or "easy." Jesus said, "For my yoke is easy and my burden is light" (Matthew 11:30). This word *easy* is the same word translated as "kindness" in Galatians. In a sense, Jesus said, "For my yoke is kind and my burden is light."

I'll give you my spin on this definition: Kindness doesn't bug you.

So when Jesus said, "My yoke is easy" or "My yoke is kind," he meant, "My yoke will not bug you. It's not going to be heavy; it's not going to be a burden; it's not going to be painful to you. It's going to be nice to you; it's going to be easy for you."

Now *goodness* has a unique meaning as well, because goodness can come only from God. We're bad. He's good. He gives His goodness to us so that we can be good to others. As with most of the fruit of the Spirit, the rubber meets the road in how we treat other people. That's where our fruit is tested. Kindness is being easy to our spouse, our kids, our brothers and sisters, and even (no, *especially*) our moms and dads. It's making things light for them. It's the opposite of bugging them. It's the opposite of adding a burden to them. It's taking some of their weight onto our shoulders, being good to them in the same way God is good to us.

Once again, you know a *great* environment for practicing kindness and goodness? Church. When it comes to making things light and easy for people, church is a great place to test our mettle. If we can run nurseries, greet visitors, run nurseries, throw fellowship dinners, run nurseries, pull off major events, and run nurseries (Did I already mention that?) while being kind and good, then we know we're producing good spiritual fruit.

Faithfulness

Faithfulness means trustworthiness and reliability. You can't have any long-term relationship without faithfulness, because if you can't trust people, you will lose confidence in them, and the relationship will deteriorate. So if you want to be the type of person who enjoys long-term relationships, you must be faithful.

How hard is that, really? Judging from divorce rates, employment histories, school dropout rates, underused health-club memberships, and debt-management issues, it must be pretty difficult. Faithfulness isn't really encouraged anywhere in our culture today; we have built cushion upon cushion for people who would rather float freely, making promises and breaking them, than have to arrange their lives to meet any kind of commitment that would inconvenience them.

Jesus was right: "Make a tree good and its fruit will be good" (Matthew 12:33). If God can make us good (and He can), then that goodness will express itself in faithfulness.

Our internship program at New Life—twentyfourseven—is a yearly experiment in faithfulness. Each year we take in dozens of high-school graduates with varying levels of faithfulness. Some are already pretty stable young men and women, but many come precisely because they sense that they're missing something, and often what they're missing is trustworthiness.

Trustworthy people are faithful; they know how to stick with something or someone worthwhile when the going gets tough, through good times and bad. So, for a year or two, we work them out. We make them get up at insane hours every morning and run for miles. We make them show up at regular prayer times, college-level classes, and Bible studies—*on time*. We make them pitch in whenever help is needed around the church or in the greater Colorado Springs community, often at a moment's notice. To do all we ask them to do, they have to learn to give of themselves completely. And they do this as a team. They have to learn to be faithful, reliable, dependable members of a community. And they do it. I love watching it happen each and every year.

We could all use a little twentyfourseven.

Gentleness

Now this is one of my favorites. Okay, they're *all* my favorites, but I have a special place for gentleness, because, depending on the day of the week, I am either the most gentle lamb in the world or the least gentle lion. Just ask my staff.

Gentleness is a gift from God. It's a timely word delivered to a hurting soul. It's a five-hundred-dollar check that arrives, without a word, from a loving family member just when the bills are overdue. It's grace and forgiveness given to someone (like, well, all of us) who deserves anything but and knows it.

People talk a lot about how President George W. Bush responded to the attacks on September 11, and they often mention his display of strength. It's true; Americans knew they had a confident, bold leader who would address the responsible parties with swift strength. But what was most impressive to me was his display of gentleness. Remember that clip of him reading "The Pet Goat" to schoolchildren as he learned of the attack on the World Trade Center? He handled the situation perfectly: By remaining calm and not reacting too quickly, he gently ushered those children into a world that he knew was about to change before their eyes.

Gentleness can do that. It can be powerful. It can be a great leadership tool. It can also be like a warm bath, a close hug, or a lazy afternoon nap. It's giving just what is needed just when it is needed, without causing a stir. It's quietly timely. It's the perfect answer. I love it.

Self-Control

This fruit involves self-mastery. This concept is referenced in Scripture in several ways, such as the self-control of an athlete who has disciplined his or her body or a Christian who has mastered immoral temptations. Self-control is overcoming your impulses so that you can get yourself to do what God wants you to do.

The apostle Paul wrote,

Who will rescue me from this body of death? Thanks be to God—through Jesus Christ our Lord!...

Therefore, there is now no condemnation for those who are in Christ Jesus, because through Christ Jesus the law of the Spirit of life set me free from the law of sin and death. (Romans 7:24-25; 8:1-2)

There is no need for failure for those who are in Christ Jesus! God has given us the ability to have self-control. This means that if your old sin nature leads to alcoholism, you need never drink another drop again for the rest of your life. Or if your old sin nature leans toward drug abuse, you need never abuse drugs again. Or if your old sin nature leans toward your being hotheaded, you need not have explosive anger in your life again.

As Christians, we should never be out of control. But we can be in control only by the mercy and grace of God.

Now the Greek word used here for "self-control" means "a powerful person"—especially in politics—"who never uses his position for self-interest." So self-control will help people master themselves so they can serve others. Do you want to be a good husband and dad? Then you have to master yourself so you can be a faithful servant to your wife and children. If you are out of control, you'll say the wrong things to them, you'll go the wrong places, you'll do the wrong things, you'll embarrass them, and you won't be a good dad. If you want to get husbanding and fathering (or anything else) right, be filled with the Holy Spirit and let self-control dominate your life.

I know you can develop some self-control with an iron will and self-discipline methods. But the best way to do it for the long haul, and with grace, is to be filled with the Holy Spirit. Remember, make a tree good, and it will produce good fruit.

Becoming a Good-Fruit Picker

Here's the exhortation from Paul that puts it all together—the sure way to become a person who produces the good fruit of the Spirit:

> Those who belong to Christ Jesus have crucified the sinful
> nature with its passions and desires. Since we live by the Spirit,
> let us keep in step with the Spirit. (Galatians 5:24-25)

All of that junk that flows so naturally from the old sin nature—anger, immorality, selfishness, envy, greed, arrogance, all of those things—has to be killed.

I have preached sermons at New Life in which I talked about the old sin nature and how we need to kill it every morning. Teenagers have come up to me afterward and said, "Ah, Pastor Ted, we really loved your talk on getting up in the morning and praying to kill our old sin nature, but we're really not even awake in the mornings. Could we pray that way in the evenings? Is it just as good?"

I answered, "Yes, it's just as good if you do it in the evening, or at midnight, or midday, or whenever. But please, for the sake of your parents, do it *once a day!*"

However, if you are not a teenager and are reasonably alert in the morning, I think starting the day with a little killing of the old sin nature is a wonderful thing—like a workout for your spiritual heart. And the secret to great early morning prayer is to turn off your television the night before. You will sleep better, and you will be more alert spiritually if you don't fill yourself up with all the garbage spewing from the screen—the hatred, foolishness, immorality, jealousy, lewdness, greed, murder, violence, lust, and other things found on the shimmering screen. Doesn't all that stuff sound like food for your sin nature? You got it. Fill up on that junk, and the next day you'll be tired. You'll oversleep, then you'll jump into your car and try to pray on the commute. That's not the kind of prayer I'm advocating in the morning—the "O God, help me!" type of prayer. I am talking about prayers that make sense, not desperate prayers you shout out as other cars are running into your car.

So the idea is to schedule your evening so that your morning works right. Then you can kill the old sin nature and put on the new.

Everyone you meet that day will be glad you picked that good fruit.

Questions for Pastor Ted

I know that I am to serve Christ by employing the gifts of the Spirit. I guess I used to look at the gifts as something God gives us to serve others. I like the thought that in serving others, in using what God's given me, I'm actually serving Christ. It really makes me feel humble. God gives us the very gifts that serve Him. There's really nothing we can do on our own, is there?

Most Christians love serving God, but when we realize that we serve God by serving others, our lives become more full. God designed the system so we can thrive on healthy relationships. A healthy relationship with God Himself through the Spirit is our core. We express service by being His representatives on earth as we serve others. He washes feet. We wash feet.

As I mature as a Christian, should I see increasing evidence of all of the fruit of the Spirit in my life? I seem to be doing better in some areas but am not seeing that much more fruit in other areas.

That's all right. God doesn't work in every area of our lives at the same time. Even though His desire is for our complete perfection, it seems as though He works in one major area at a time, and then, once that area is refined, He begins to work on another area.

Let me tell you a story that shows how God works with us. I knew three high-school brothers from a non-Christian family. Before these three guys came to Christ, they were all sexually immoral, were drinkers, and loved to smoke pot. Interestingly, even though the three brothers received Christ at the same time, God worked differently in each of them.

Immediately upon conversion, one boy met with his girlfriend to tell her that they could not sleep together anymore because of his new commitment to Christ. He wanted to be sexually pure. However, he wasn't immediately convicted about other issues.

The second brother wasn't concerned about his immoral relationship with his girlfriend at all. Instead, he never drank another drop of alcohol. He never wanted to get drunk again. He announced it to his friends, refused to go to drinking parties, and made a strong statement about the importance of good Christians not abusing alcohol.

I know you can already guess what I'm about to say. Yes, the third brother kept his relationship with his girlfriend and enjoyed drinking a beer or two with his buddies, but he threw out all of his marijuana and started preaching to his brothers that they were missing it big time by not getting rid of their weed as well.

In time all three boys were cleaned up by the Holy Spirit and lived pure lives without sex, drugs, or alcohol. But until they all had made these changes, which took several years, they fought with one another. They couldn't understand why their brothers didn't clean up the same way they had. You might be asking the same question. I have the answer: It's the way the Holy Spirit works. He illuminates and cleanses our lives individually and often uniquely.

So don't be worried that some of your spiritual gifts are stronger than others or that some fruit is more evident than other fruit. And don't be dismayed if another genuine Christian has a different walk than you do. Instead, read your Bible and pray every day. Remember to kill the old sin nature in your morning prayer time, and let the life of God grow in you. As you do, He'll remove the old and will refresh and fill you, and you'll find yourself growing steadily.

One note: A time of prayer and fasting is a great way to jump-start your spiritual growth. If you are stagnant and slow in your spiritual growth, go somewhere alone with your Bible and spend three days praying and fasting. You'll rest and refresh physically and be empowered spiritually. You might not notice much spiritual progress while you are praying and fasting, but you will notice a profound difference afterward. Go find God, and let Him go to work in you!

Twelve

DIG FOR DIAMONDS

As we have learned throughout this book, all of us were born with an old sin nature. There is a garbage dump at the core of human existence, and it's inside each one of us.

If you are not born again, and you want to find peace, power, and purpose by digging down into yourself through excessive introspection and self-help techniques, good luck! When you get to the core, you are going to find corruption, hatred, lust, jealousy, selfishness, and more. It smells down there.

Now because a human being is fearfully and wonderfully made in the image of God (see Psalm 139:14), you will see some very nice things too—mostly near the surface. Many parents do a good job of training their children, and a good education helps, and through various life experiences all of us have learned a lot of appropriate behavior. But none of that provides the power to really change the core of our being.

But if you are born again, the story is totally different. When you became fully aware of your need to change, you acknowledged your need for God, for the forgiveness of sins, and for the cleansing power of the Holy Spirit. You made a great decision and accepted Jesus as Lord and Savior.

So if you could dig to the core of someone regenerated by God, rather than finding a corroded old sin nature, you would find a beautiful diamond—a precious stone that represents all the gifts, traits, blessings, and fruit of God. Everything made available to those who are His children.

After we are reborn and filled with the Spirit, God begins the process of revealing the diamond He has placed at our core. Through our responsiveness to God's Word, which reveals the gospel, along with our obedience to His Spirit, He transforms us into who He wants us to be. Because we live in a fallen world and because of our own fallenness, we endure all kinds of suffering and anxiety as we learn to throw ourselves into the arms of Christ. This is not like whizzing through a spiritual drive-through lane. It's definitely a process.

The Bible calls this process a "walk," a long walk that will last for the rest of our lives. When you begin the walk, it appears that there's only a slight glimmer of a diamond inside you, and the rest is still junk. But as you study the Scriptures, grow in the Spirit, and participate in His body, the church, more and more of the diamond is revealed. You experience healing and deliverance and many other wonderful things. You overcome more and more as the kingdom of God increasingly dominates your life.

That's why we seek the Lord in prayer, fasting, and worship. All of these good actions chip away at the rough outer crust of the old sin nature to reveal the core diamond and its many beautiful facets.

Daily experiences—even failures—help the process along. Remember that last speeding ticket? How did you respond to the situation? You may not see it this way, but when a police officer stops you and says, "You were going twenty miles over the speed limit. License and registration," God is trying to expose your diamond just a little bit more and get rid of some more of the old sin-nature stuff that's still there.

Or if you are in your prayer closet, pacing back and forth as you seek the Lord and not sensing the presence of God, when you hang in there and keep at it, you are doing your part in digging out the diamond. You are saying, "I want the righteousness of God. I want the kingdom of God to dominate in me."

Or if you fail at something and are so disappointed with what you've said or done, you have a chance to respond—to be humble, to seek God's forgiveness, to uncover a little bit more of the diamond.

You will meet Christians who think we can unveil the diamond by obedience to the law and by following rules and regulations. Sorry, but that just isn't going to happen. It's the Holy Spirit living within us who imparts righteousness and empowers the Word of God in our lives. Christianity is all about a vital and dynamic relationship with God, who has sent His Holy Spirit to guide us into that relationship.

All of the things we choose to do or not do are an expression of our intimate, covenant relationship with God. We tithe not to win the favor of God but to demonstrate our relationship with Him. We come to church not to earn the right to a relationship with God—that was appropriated on the cross—but to get to know Him more. We do important things in our Christian walk in order to dig out our diamonds, because we desperately long to grow in the Lord, to have a healthy, dynamic relationship with Him.

GOD ENJOYS RELATIONSHIP

The Trinity gives us a great example of how God likes to do relationships.

I love getting a glimpse of the interaction between the Father, Son, and Holy Spirit. We see this when John baptized Jesus at the Jordan River. Heaven opened, the Holy Spirit descended on Jesus like a dove, and the voice of God the Father burst through the clouds, proclaiming admiration and delight for His Son.

Literally out of the blue, the Father broke into time and space and said, "That's My boy! I'm so pleased with Him!" (see Luke 3:22). If this happened today, He would say something like, "Look at Him! That's My boy, and I love everything about Him."

So this is the picture we see: God is in love with His Son, the Son lives to glorify His Father, and the Holy Spirit is flowing between them. They're talking with one another, loving one another, blessing one another, doing miracles with one another—it's a remarkably delightful relationship.

And we need to pay attention to what this means for us.

God created us in His own image and likeness, so like any kid, we have many of the same character qualities as our Dad. That means when it comes to relationships, we have a deep desire to connect with others. We love laughing with, eating with, playing with, and just plain hanging out with good friends. It doesn't matter where you go, human beings all over the world—regardless of background, race, language, nationality, or religion—devise ways of connecting with other people. It's just what humans do.

But there's a problem with all of this desire to connect: Our intimate, ideal relationship with God has been severed by our sinful independence, and this same old sin nature works to destroy our relationships with other people. Too many relationships are stained with difficult things like rejection, inappropriate affection, dysfunctional patterns of relating in families, high divorce rates, broken lives—on and on it goes. The very thing people want most—rich, loving personal relationships—seems out of their grasp.

POWERFUL RELATIONSHIPS

As we close our discussion of the message in Galatians, I want to offer some final observations about relationships. How can we have wonderful, powerful, loving relationships with God and others in the body of Christ?

The relational dynamic with God is mysterious, personal, intimate, lively, and vibrant. Some days it's effervescent; other days it's serious. There are times in our relationship with God when we want to worship Him radically, to explode with adoration for Him. Other times we're drawn to lie on our faces and be still in His presence. Some days He wants us to get out of the prayer room and go do something. Other days He wants us to stop being busybodies and sit down and chill out. Don't ask me why He wants what He wants. The Christian life involves a mysterious, relational dynamic with a loving God, and lots of people have trouble navigating its ambiguities. But we are like Him, and He is like us—more than we might think.

So if we want to understand God and live as He intends, we must understand personal relationships. If we think relationships are systematic and orderly, we can forget it. There are too many variables. God's heart is a mystery. So is ours.

Near the end of his letter, Paul had some insights on how this understanding of relationships helps us function better in the church:

> Brothers, if someone is caught in a sin, you who are spiritual
> should restore him gently. But watch yourself, or you also may

be tempted. Carry each other's burdens, and in this way you
will fulfill the law of Christ. If anyone thinks he is something
when he is nothing, he deceives himself. Each one should test
his own actions. Then he can take pride in himself, without
comparing himself to somebody else, for each one should
carry his own load. (Galatians 6:1-5)

The number-one measure of our character is how we learn to
manage ourselves—our thought lives, our physical being, our affec-
tions, and the issues we have with acceptance and rejection.

The second greatest test or indicator of our character is our
response to someone else's sin. We tend to understand and accept our
own struggles, but we don't always have that much grace for the difficulties of others. I think that's why the apostle Paul brought up this
topic right after he talked about the works of the flesh and the fruit of
the Spirit. After helping us understand ourselves, Paul immediately
moved on to discuss our relationships with others.

He said that we have a duty to help our fallen brothers and sisters
get back on their feet again (see verse 1). When we are exhorted in the
Spirit to correct a person who has fallen, we are supposed to repair
him or her. In Greek, the word Paul used is the same one that
describes a surgeon doing his work. In other words, helping someone
recover from sin is like setting a broken arm or taking out a tumor; it
involves time, precision, and care. So when someone gets into trouble,
we shouldn't panic. God understands and has provided a way to bring
healing and restoration. The issue is, how will we respond? Will we
calmly make repairs like a surgeon? Or will we blast like a linebacker
through people and their needs?

The issue of handling someone's sin and correcting that person is tricky. It's a matter of curing, not punishing. When people get entangled in their old sin nature, our old sin nature wants to lay down the law and punish them. But if they are born again, then we have to trust that the diamond is there. The issue is getting the muck cleaned away from the diamond.

And what about our own muck? We are all dealing with sin constantly. The execution of our old sin natures cannot be fully accomplished just by ourselves. Sometimes we need an entire firing squad with plenty of ammunition.

We've already discussed how important it is to go in the prayer closet by ourselves and crucify the old sin nature, put on Christ, and live a godly, wholesome, overcoming, victorious life. We must do that. Like Paul, we need to die daily. But how can others help us? What kinds of relationships will best help to expose and polish our diamond within?

All of us have what I call passive relationships. These are not energetic, connected, powerful relationships that make you smile or weep. They are just *there*. The mood of such relationships is reminiscent of worshiping some idol—which I'm not recommending—as opposed to worshiping the living God. The whole deal is lifeless and lame.

Sometimes I call these relationships "cordial relationships," the kind of relationships that amount to surfacy conversation:

"Hi, how are you?"

"Fine, thanks. And how's everything with you?"

"Oh, it's great, thanks."

"Good to see you."

"Nice to see you. I like your hair."

"Thanks. Well, gotta go. You take care! Let's get together sometime."

"Sure. Bye!"

And both of you know the chance of your getting together is as likely as George Bush asking you to spend the weekend hanging out at Camp David.

Such encounters are a little awkward because the relationship is passive, and you don't really know what to do with it. Maybe something might come of it, but for now you wouldn't want to go on vacation with this person, and you might avoid a lunch date, too.

This passive relationship issue is everywhere. Some people have nothing but passive relationships. Worse, many married couples find themselves stuck in a passive state. They are cordial and nice, but they never really empower each other. That means that lots of kids grow up in homes where they never see or experience true connection.

Don't get me wrong. Life is full of cordial surface relationships, and that's normal. We shouldn't be rude and ignore people, and we shouldn't force everyone to be our best friends.

But there's a different kind of relationship that I think is God's plan for diamond polishing. I call it a "power relationship," or a dynamic connection. God designed us to connect with Him by the power of the Holy Spirit, and it's the power of that connectivity that changes our lives. He gives us power through His relationship with us, and we change.

The same type of thing happens between people. When people learn to powerfully connect with other people in a family, in close friendships, and in a body of believers, they establish life-giving, positive relationships that empower them in their spirits to be everything God wants them to be.

So to stomp the living daylights out of the old sin nature, you need both a vibrant personal relationship with God *and* vibrant connectivity with others in the body of believers. This is what a life-giving church is! It's an *ecclesia*—a gathering together of the brethren. It's how we strengthen one another to live life and fulfill our purposes.

Men have the desire to have men friends, and women have the desire to have women friends. Groups of people love getting together and engaging one another. There is supernatural strength in loyal, faithful friends, and that strength helps human beings become everything God created them to be.

I am mentioning this because you may be a person who loves God with all of your heart, and yet you live a disconnected life. One way to measure this is to ask yourself, "Are there nights when I wake up scared and lonely and don't have anybody to share those feelings with?" The times when you have sobbed the most deeply, have you sobbed alone? The times when you have become insecure and wondered about your own adequacy, was there no one to talk with because you feared that if someone really got to know you, he or she would reject you?

If that describes your life, I want you to know that it's not God's plan for you. He wants you connected to Him in a loving, vibrant relationship, and He wants you connected to others.

Again, this is why I am such a fan of small groups in the local church. In the small-group setting, people have the opportunity to find personal connectivity to others, which is so critical to spiritual growth and success. At New Life Church, we have Free Market small groups. This means that anyone in the church who wants to lead a small group—on almost any topic—is encouraged to do so. Of course, every leader must go through a training session and express agreement with the basics of the faith and the philosophy of the church. But beyond that, they are free to do their own thing with others who want to join them.

We do this because we want people to be involved in more than powerless, passive, cordial relationships. In powerful, dynamic relationships, people will invest in one another's lives so significantly that the greatest fear won't win, the besetting sin won't conquer.

I've observed that it's possible to spend years in a church and never really connect. Sure, it's important to get together in a large group to worship, learn, and share the sacraments. But if we stop with that, we miss the point: Fellowship with God and connectivity with one another exist so that we can empower one another for the perfect plan God has for us.

So just what did Paul mean when he said we should "gently" restore those caught in sin (Galatians 6:1)? He meant that when you find somebody in trouble, if you are dealing with your old sin nature in prayer, are being filled with the Holy Spirit, are growing in faith, and have vital connections to God and other believers, you can reach into the life of someone who needs help and pull that person up so that his strengths—not his afflicting weaknesses—define his life.

Paul also said that we need to do this with great humility, avoiding conceit. It's another take on Jesus's idea of always taking the log out of one's own eye before taking the splinter out of someone else's eye. If we are not careful, we will see people struggling and think, *Man, I am living a pretty good life. I am doing all right. Look at all these other poor strugglers—they're really messing up!*

Paul says, "Don't do that. Don't compare yourselves with others. It's not relevant, and it doesn't accomplish anything positive. It will just make you conceited, which means you, too, will soon be messing up."

Instead, we should test our own actions (see Galatians 6:4) by comparing ourselves to where God wants us to be. This will keep us healthy and make us strong.

How do we gauge whether we are connecting with others? We know we're doing it when...

- we have a good group of friends around us.
- we know how to pray for one another.
- we know how to protect and edify one another.
- we know how to grow old together.
- we know how to encourage and coach one another.
- we know how to keep distance when distance is right, and how to be close when close is right.
- we have learned the skills of good living.

In the midst of that kind of life, when someone gets in trouble, rather than saying, "Oh, what is she doing? She must not have it together," we are able to say, "I want to help. I can give her some strength. I can connect with her in this. I can share her suffering. I can cry with her if she needs somebody to cry with. I can love her when she needs somebody to love her. I can be faithful to her when she needs somebody to be faithful to her. I can connect with her and help her overcome these difficulties."

When you connect with people and infuse them with strength, life, joy, and peace, you are finding the diamond inside of them. You are choosing to chip away at that outer crust to find the diamond instead of the crud, highlighting the good instead of focusing on the dirty sin parts.

That's what God wants the body of Christ to be like, and that can't happen if we live according to the law. That's what Paul is arguing here. He wants us to be so connected with one another that life flows powerfully between us. This is the choice you and I make. If someone falls into a sin, let us, in humility, connect with him and build him up by highlighting the righteousness of Christ in him.

A FRIEND IN DEED

This whole issue of connecting with other people is so important, I want to tell you about an unusual incident in my life that illustrates the value of a friend and how all this can work.

I was in my office a few years ago, suffering with a really bad cold. I felt awful. It was one of those sniffling, sneezing, terrible sore throat, whining, crying, weeping, moaning kind of days. I ached all over. I was a mess.

Okay, so you're thinking, *You poor baby, Ted. You were whining and crying about a simple cold?*

I was. I admit it. I may seem like a spiritual giant on Sundays, all dressed up, with the fire of God shooting from my lips, but a rotten head cold turns me into a sniveling wimp. And when I get sick, I am very moody. It's just pathetic! I think the White House should close, Congress should recess, the military should stand down—everything should stop. When I get sick, it's all about "Take care of me" and "I am the only one in the world."

So there I was—an emotional, self-focused, pitiful mess—sitting at my desk, longing for the Second Coming, when my friend Patton Dodd walked in. Patton has helped me with my writing over the years, and he was stopping by to go over a project. When he saw me, he asked, "Oh my, what's wrong with you?"

I looked at him with bleary eyes and said, "I can't go home. I've got work to do, but o-o-o-h-h-h-h!" I fell speechless, consumed by my pain.

Instead of laughing or running away, Patton said, "You look terrible."

I nodded my head and wiped my nose with a tissue.

"Why don't you just sit on the couch for a little bit," he suggested.

I sighed and shuffled over to the couch in my office, where I slumped down into a heap.

You should know that Patton is a young man, but he really has relational maturity. He's a deep-water guy with a quiet spirit.

Anyway, there I was sitting on the couch and moaning, and Patton was nearby in a chair wanting to discuss some work with me. But he could tell I was spaced out—totally enmeshed in despair. So instead of excusing himself or trying to get something out of me, Patton came over and sat down on the other end of the couch. He didn't say anything. He just sat next to me. We both just sat there for a long while, not saying anything.

Lost in head-cold misery, I kept feeling bad for myself—aching, whining, wheezing, coughing, sneezing. Patton didn't say a word. He just sat there with me.

We sat there quietly, and the longer this went on, the better I felt. Oh, I still had my lousy cold, but I appreciated so much someone just being there. If he had started to chat, I probably would have gone home. If he had tried to pep me up with some superspiritual truism such as "God will use this in your life," I would have hated it. If he had tried to tell me about some new, modern snake-oil cold-relief potion, I would have thought, *Man, I have taken so much of that stuff already that I can't see straight.*

But he didn't do or say anything. He just sat there, and in that way, he let me know he was there for me. I appreciated it.

Finally, after a while, he said, "Okay, Pastor Ted, it's time for you to go home." That was it!

So I went home.

That kind of connectivity brought me comfort when I needed it. Patton didn't leave me alone in my misery. Instead, by quietly sitting next to me on the couch, he was saying, "I'm here for you; lean on my strength."

I've also felt the strength of my friends when I have been on the verge of making a mistake, when I start thinking a little too highly of myself, or when my thinking is skewed. And when I'm on the right track, they're also there to help me fulfill the vision and purpose God has given me. I can't imagine my life apart from being connected to the body of Christ.

Those who live life without connectivity, well, they never fully run the race, jump as high as they could, go as far as they could, or experience the full power of God as they should.

That's why I want to encourage you to connect with other believers and develop good, close friends. They help us in the process of chipping away at our sinful nature to uncover that diamond within us.

The apostle Paul understood this. Even though he had been a father to the Galatian believers by bringing the gospel to them, he experienced the strength of their love for him during the trial of his illness. Now he was returning that love by passionately defending the true gospel he had preached to them, which alone had the power to set them free and bring them into right relationship with God. He wanted to protect them from the trap of believing that obedience to the law would earn them justification in God's sight.

This gospel—that Christ gave Himself for our sins so that we can receive our total justification through faith in Him—is the power that breaks us out of our bondage to sin and sets us free to become sons and daughters of God, in right relationship with Him and with each other.

It's the power that enables us to be foolish no more!

Questions for Pastor Ted

I'm in a marriage in which my wife and I have a pretty passive relationship. What can I do to make things better?

Suggest to your spouse that you pick out a book on marriage, sex, relationships, or whatever interests the two of you, and read it together. I suggest you read a page or two to your spouse, then have him or her read some to you. Do it regularly together, and you'll notice that your life as a couple is improving. Also start saying a little prayer together before you fall asleep at night. These two things will work more effectively if you remember to be nice to each other!

Sometimes people treat a stranger at the grocery store nicer than they do the members of their own family. If this describes you, *stop it!* Be cordial, be nice, and don't wound people. If you feel hurt and are hurting others, get help and healing. If you are wounded and disappointed and, because of it, are harsh with your wife and children, get help and get healed. No matter what the issues are, go get help and find healing. Pray and fast, talk with some good friends or a good pastor, and, if necessary, see a counselor. But don't be mean and nasty! These seeds will destroy you.

Finally, be sure your sex life is good with your spouse. Lots of people who have a passive marriage have either no sex with their spouse or lousy sex. This is not God's plan. If you are into pornography or masturbation, are using prostitutes, or are having extramarital sex of any kind, this stuff is poisoning you and your marriage. One hundred percent of your sex life should be with your spouse. If it's not, your deficient intimacy will weaken your entire relationship. Improve your sex life with your spouse. Work on your sex life with your spouse. Talk honestly and openly—then work together to improve things.

Lots of married couples are weak in this area because they want to stay "pure" or more focused on God. But in their efforts to stay pure, they don't have a marriage that works. Bottom line: Our marriage relationship represents Christ (the husband) and the church (the bride). Intimacy in marriage is meaningful because it is the picture of Christ and the church. To mismanage this area of our lives is to invite ruin in every other area. So have fun! Grow together! Enjoy each other!

Don't neglect some common-sense issues: If you are too fat, lose weight so you can enjoy each other more. If you are out of shape, hit the gym so you can enjoy each other again. If you are a bad lover, learn to be a good one. Don't forsake each other, but instead, enjoy each other as God intended.

About the Author

TED HAGGARD is president of the thirty million–member National Association of Evangelicals (NAE), the largest evangelical group in America. He is also founder and senior pastor of the eleven thousand–member New Life Church in Colorado Springs, Colorado.

Ted founded and serves as the president of both the Association of Life-Giving Churches, a network of local churches, and *world prayerteam.org,* the only real-time global prayer network. He is also the author of seven books, including the best-selling *Primary Purpose.*

Ted and his wife, Gayle, live in Colorado Springs with their five children.

For more information, visit the following Web sites:

- New Life Church: *www.newlifechurch.org*
- The National Association of Evangelicals: *www.nae.net*
- The Association of Life-Giving Churches: *www.lifegiving church.org*
- World Prayer Team: *www.worldprayerteam.org*

Find *JOY* as your husband's partner in ministry

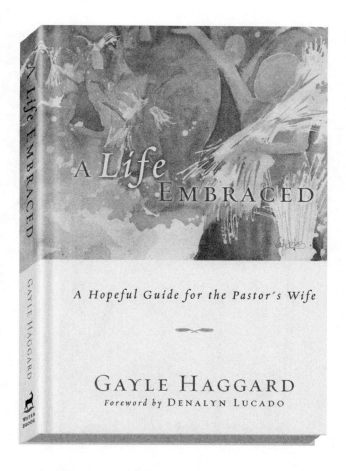

Available in bookstores and from online retailers

www.waterbrookpress.com